# AUTOBIOGRAPHY OF DYING

# AUTOBIOGRAPHY
# OF
# DYING

## Archie J. Hanlan

*Postscript by Mary S. Hanlan*

EDITED BY MURIEL E. NELSON

Doubleday & Company, Inc.
Garden City, New York
1979

LIBRARY OF CONGRESS CATALOGING IN PUBLICATION DATA
Hanlan, Archie J.
Autobiography of Dying.

1. Amyotrophic lateral sclerosis—Biography.
2. Death—Psychological aspects.
3. Hanlan, Archie. I. Title.
RC406.A24H36     362.1'9'83
ISBN: 0-385-14481-4
Library of Congress Catalog Card Number 78-7755

To Grandpa Jim,
who shared Daddy's warmth and love of life

Marc

Lori

Jim

# Contents

---

## ∼ EDITOR'S PREFACE

This book is about the anguishing and the mundane, the frustrating and the tolerable, the strange and the familiar experiences one man had in living with the prospect of his early death. The man was Archie Hanlan, who died in July 1973 at the age of forty-eight, the victim of the steady progression of a condition called "Lou Gehrig's disease," or "ALS" (amyotrophic lateral sclerosis).

Although he began recording in 1971, only a few details seem "dated." On the contrary, the book is part of a current surge of popular, scientific, and semiscientific writing and teaching on death and dying. ("D and D," as one hears it from the *cognoscenti*, is presumably becoming yet another specialized field.) Countering the harmful effect of our society's marked tendency to isolate the dying patient, a kind of denial that death occurs, much attention is now being given to personal accounts of the dying experience. Each has its uniqueness, as does this one.

Archie Hanlan was a teacher of social work. After taking his master's degree in social welfare at the University of California at Berkeley in 1956, he worked in public child-welfare and mental-health programs. Though he moved on into supervision and administration, he maintained a small private practice. Later he returned to the university and in 1967 became a Doctor of Social Welfare. His teaching career began at Berkeley, extended to Washington University's George Warren Brown School of Social Work, in St. Louis, and included a visiting professorship at the University of Arkansas one summer. In 1970 he joined the faculty of the University of Pennsylvania's Graduate School of Social Work as associate professor. There he was chosen to be director of a new social administration program, aiming to engage several schools at the university in studying methods of administering such large-scale human-service organizations as occur in medicine, education, and the social services.

His academic publications include:

(1) "From Social Reform to Social Security: The Separation of ADC and Child Welfare," *Child Welfare*, Vol. XLV, No. 9 (November 1966)

(2) "Counteracting Problems of Bureaucracy in Public Welfare," *Social Work* 12:88 (July 1967)

(3) "Public Welfare, Civil Rights, and Human Rights," *Public Welfare* 27:1 (January 1969)

(4) "Social Work and Private Industry," with Sydney Jacobs, *Social Casework* 50:3 (March 1969)

(5) "From Social Work to Social Administration." In *Social Work Practice*, National Conference on Social Welfare (New York: Columbia University Press, 1970)

(6) "Casework Beyond Bureaucracy," *Social Casework* 52:4 (April 1971)

(7) "Changing Functions and Structures." In Florence Kaslow et al., *Issues in Human Services* (San Francisco: Jossey-Bass, Inc., 1972)

In each city, he had community interests and responsibilities, such as serving as consultant to a Model Cities program and to new schools of social work, hosting regular "rap sessions" with students in his home, and participating in study and action for needed change.

Since his family could not immediately move to Philadelphia with him, he lived initially as a faculty adviser in a new dormitory and returned about once a month to St. Louis. By the first winter, he found himself exhausted, unable to carry a suitcase in his right hand. A medical examination revealed no problems. For the rest of the story, we have the diary and articles that follow.

His career uniquely qualified Dr. Hanlan to portray his world in depth. He was trained to observe people and experienced in doing so, both in their psychobiological functioning and in their interaction. His professional discipline required that he also observe himself, identify his own motivations and biases, and search out his subjective impulses and reactions to use as tools; it further required that he direct these into useful channels, as he did with this book. With the rest of humankind, he had a few blind spots, some of which will be apparent to the reader. Though determined and persistent, he was highly responsive to challenge, as is seen particularly in the dialogues with students and teachers.

An expert in helping people, he knew the dilemmas of the helper, even as he was keenly sensitive to faults and problems in the process. In handling some of his own problems, he called upon social workers and confirmed his respect for that kind of help. Withal, he sought for others what he wanted for himself. He challenged medical professionals with the deficiencies in their service, both individual and institutional. As he lived with his terminal illness, he was increasingly critical of the famous Kübler-Ross theories, though he admired her concern for and attention to the dying person's needs.

Some of Dr. Hanlan's writings on dying are now being used in the training of physicians, nurses, dentists, and social workers. This book also will have obvious value for such people. However, it may be equally useful to the more usual readers of books about life. Death is, as he put it in the diary, a part of life. Even if we know this, despite the denial around us, we may know it in more usable terms when we have read his book.

When Mary Hanlan, his widow, found that she was unable to manage the editing and promotion of the book, I was glad to try my hand. As a former colleague, I valued Dr. Hanlan's thinking and shared his concerns. I also thought the work might do something for me—perhaps fill some of the gaps in facing my own mortality and that of others, perhaps even help me reconcile to the loss of Archie Hanlan himself, a dear and respected friend.

I agreed almost completely with Dr. Hanlan's ideas for the contents of the book. For readability, I felt we must now eliminate most of the repetition that had occurred in the course of using the material. I chose the diary itself over the published versions. While it required much editing, I thought the journal form had its own merit, in that the observations and ideas appeared as they emerged, sometimes accompanied by anger, petulance, or confusion but still thoughtful and thought-provoking, as he developed and integrated his experience along the way. So I made changes that were essentially minor, for clarity and smoothness only, almost always preserving Dr. Hanlan's words and phrases. Then I included as footnotes parts of the published articles and, in both footnotes and Appendix, parts of the unpublished transcripts, but only when they provided a slant that seemed to enhance the diary.

I am sure Dr. Hanlan would have applauded our adding his wife's keen, articulate paper, written in the second year after his death.

The title of the book is Dr. Hanlan's. I named the chapters, partly as a guide to the editing. The footnotes are mine.

Whoever transcribed his tapes did a masterful job. I think particularly of the ones done in February 1973, when his speech was sorely impaired.

I, too, have been helped in working on this book, not only by Mary Hanlan but by three other friends, social work colleagues: Esther Fibush, Trudi Selznick, and Winifred Thomas. Many thanks to these sound thinkers and consultants.

In reading for my task, I have realized that Dr. Hanlan would welcome some of the recent developments that further the cause of dying people. I think especially of these books: Kastenbaum and Aisenberg's comprehensive work *The Psychology of Death;* Milton D. Heifetz's *The Right to Die;* May Sarton's short novel from the viewpoint of a convalescent home resident *As We Are Now;* and Robert E. Neale's *The Art of Dying.* There are many more. He would be encouraged that the hospice movement, developed in England, is beginning to take hold in the United States; that ethics is now high on the agenda of medical groups; that an ALS (amyotrophic lateral sclerosis) foundation has emerged in New York; and that legislation on the rights of patients is being enacted.

I have learned important things from this modest book. I take pleasure now in helping it to reach others. Here it is, substantially as prepared in 1971 to 1973, *Autobiography of Dying,* by Archie J. Hanlan, D.S.W.

Muriel E. Nelson, A.C.S.W.
October 1977

P.S. Having properly established Dr. Hanlan's academic status and title, I now rejoin the many people who affectionately called him "Archie."

M.N.

# ~ INTRODUCTION

The purpose of this introduction is threefold: (1) to recount how this book came about, (2) to identify the connections and progression of my writings on death and dying and how they form a coherent whole, and (3) to acknowledge some of the many people without whom the book would have been impossible.

I am writing with awareness that I will never know if the book reaches the point of publication. Although I strongly hope that it does, the experience itself has been more than worth the time-and-energy investment. I decided to embark on the project sometime during the summer of 1971, several months after I was told that I had an incurable, progressive illness. Knowing the peculiar nature of my disease, that my body would wither away while my mind remained intact, I thought of Bruno Bettelheim's effort to preserve his sanity in a Nazi concentration camp. Perhaps engaging myself in an intellectual analysis of what was happening to me would help keep me motivated and would capitalize on my custom of using intellectual activity as a major means of maintaining my psychological well-being. So I began to maintain a weekly diary by means of a tape recorder.

Soon I learned that a colleague, Dr. Abraham Schmitt, was offering an interdisciplinary seminar on death and dying at the University in the fall semester. I told him of my illness and offered to speak to the students at some point. He arranged for me to come in December. Then, at the seminar, I used some of the recorded material from my diary.

Sometime later, Mr. Anthony Lyle, editor of the *Pennsylvania Gazette*, told me he had heard a tape recording of my lecture and would like me to consider having it published. The article, published anonymously, resulted in wide, positive response, which further encouraged me to pursue the idea of a book.

Materials for the book comprise several published and unpublished articles and the tape-recorded diary, which was completed in April 1972. While I have not gone back over the recording, I am sure it still accurately reflects my thoughts and feelings. Although there may be both gaps and overlaps among these materials, I think that in their entirety they do convey a sense of my view of death and dying, and, more important, of living under difficult circumstances.

I make few references in this book to original sources and authors. My intellectual debt is greatest to the work of Erik Erikson, Erving Goffman, and the late Lydia Rapoport, professor of social work at Berkeley. These people show very little in common, but I have borrowed many of their ideas and have found these compatible in my professional and personal life. I have found psychoanalytic theory to be especially helpful for my own self-analysis, but I remain exceedingly critical of the state of that theory and would not impose it upon others. Similarly, the symbolic interactionists, especially Goffman, have provided me with a vital social perspective, of which I nevertheless remain critical mainly because it tends to discount much of psychology's contribution.

Whatever the labor on my part to produce this book, it also reflects the labor and love of my family: my wife, Mary, and my children, Marc, Lori, and Jim. There are many people who have made the effort possible. They include Gertrude Copperman, M.D., Reuben Copperman, M.D., Sydney and Sylvia Jacobs, Hace Tishler, Rufus Lynch, Toni Groomes, Paul and Deirdre Katz, Shirley and Bill Kahn; and California friends, who wrote special letters: Irene Prince Harmon, Hazel Bearss, and Muriel Nelson.* I am sure I have omitted acknowledging the help and love given to me by many people, but they will know who they are.

*Archie Hanlan*
*July 1973*

---

* Elsewhere, Mr. Hanlan has published this note: "I want to publicly acknowledge the editorial help . . . of Mr. Anthony Lyle. . . . Mr. Lyle has exercised unusual sensitivity and acute judgment in the preparation of these articles." (*Pennsylvania Gazette*, February 1973, page 32.)

# ARCHIE HANLAN'S DIARY

"Death seems easy, but dying . . . seems impossible."
*Archie Hanlan*

# CHAPTER ONE

# Becoming a Patient

---

It began very innocently, this era of my life. I complained to my wife about a mild weakness in my right hand, hoping she might agree that it was not worth making a doctor's appointment. On the other hand, I was somewhat frightened at this strange, small symptom, and she, sensing my anxiety, urged me to make the appointment. That was the beginning of a series of events, six months ago, that have yet to reach their inevitable conclusion.

In January I had had a thorough annual checkup by our physician in the Midwest, with a clean bill of health. Now, in March, I returned to him with this silly complaint. For several weeks I had noticed that it was very difficult for me to trim my fingernails with a nail clipper held in my right hand. Also, carrying a briefcase in the right hand was becoming increasingly burdensome. Hearing of these symptoms in his office, my doctor suggested that perhaps it was some form of osteoarthritis. He thought I should see an orthopedist within a week. Possibly some minor surgery would be necessary to clear up the trouble in the right hand. He urged that I not postpone seeing an orthopedist.

The earliest available appointment with this bone specialist was the following week. While I have never had a stunning memory, I vividly recall seeing the orthopedist on a Thursday afternoon. After a few minutes of examination, his serious expression and unwillingness to discuss the symptoms said a great deal. He made it clear that I should see a neurologist soon, on that same day if it was possible.

As I returned to my wife in the orthopedist's waiting room, the grimness of my feelings at that point must have conveyed itself immediately to her. Bypassing all her pressing chores, including dinner for the children, my wife waited for me for a very long while in the office of the neurologist. By about seven o'clock that night I was finally admitted to an examining room for the first of many neurological examinations.

I had had something of a stereotyped view of neurologists before these encounters. In my clinical training as a social worker I occasionally trained and practiced with psychiatrists and psychoanalysts. Somewhere along the line I picked up the notion of the neurologist as a kind of prima donna in the medical specializations, who often was intellectually and technically brilliant at the same time that he was emotionally unable to relate to people and unable to deal with his own feelings.

Unfortunately for me, this stereotype was borne out in that neurologist's office on that Thursday night. Wearing a weary, masklike face, the neurologist gave me very little information and actually spoke as little as possible. This had the effect of increasing my anxiety during the examination to an almost intolerable level. This reached a crescendo when, at the very last moment, the neurologist told me in cryptic terms that I would be hospitalized the following morning if he could find a bed for me.*

---

\* Editor's note: The following comments Archie made about this experience appeared in "Notes of a Dying Professor," published anonymously by the *Pennsylvania Gazette*, March 1972.

I said I wanted to know why I was going to the hospital. He said: To run a series of diagnostic tests. I did not want to go to the particular hospital he mentioned. I knew that hospital very well and I had a preference for another one. But he did not practice in that hospital, so I did not pursue it. The point I want to make clear is that I began to respond to his directive to be hospitalized. I didn't know what in the

I was dismissed from his examining room, to hear from his secretary in the morning about when I could be hospitalized.

I returned once more to my wife in the waiting room. The fact of going into the hospital only seemed numbing to us by this time. Obviously, some serious, possibly dread, disease was suspected, but also obviously, we were not going to learn anything from the physicians who had dealt with me thus far.

Although I was prepared to enter the hospital on the following morning, a Friday, it was not until Friday afternoon that the neurologist's secretary told me that no hospital beds were available until Saturday. Saturday noon, then, I began to be processed as a patient. And before I was discharged, I was processed as a dying patient.

In the efficient office of admissions, I quickly began to feel that I was perceived as something more of an object than a person. In a very matter-of-fact way, I was required to assure the hospital that I would pay the full bill before I was discharged. I not only resented the financial insanity of this position, but I was increasingly furious at the total dis-

---

world I was being hospitalized for. I was not unwilling to be hospitalized, but I certainly had a particular choice of hospitals.

But suddenly I felt this fear and panic and kind of being put in a position of passivity, as though decisions were being made for me, that I didn't take part in those any more. What right did I have to make a big issue of what hospital I was being sent to?

Under ordinary circumstances, I would have made such a stink. What is significant is that I didn't. I did not feel able to fight even at that point. And this was only the first day of my discovering that something was radically wrong with me. I mention this because that process—feeling myself reduced in making decisions about my own fate—became increasingly reinforced and became very destructive psychologically.

regard for me as a human being. Suddenly I was being defined unequivocally as a patient, different from all people who manage patients.

And I managed to refuse to sign such a statement. I didn't know how much money it would take, or whether I had that amount. It was ridiculous. They scurried around to find a supervisor who could approve admission anyhow.

Next, even though I could walk well, I was put into a wheelchair and wheeled to the ward that became my home, a living hell, for the next seven days. (I suppose patients are more easily managed by being wheeled about. The message is strong: be passive!)

For several hours, I was unaware that this floor was not the usual one for a patient who was to undergo his first series of extensive diagnostic examinations. Eventually, I learned that I was there simply because of overcrowding on the usual floor. Meanwhile, I was reacting with horror to what I saw. Most of the patients were speechless, staring, grunting, disheveled men whose neurosurgery had been unsuccessful. I had seen hundreds of lobotomized patients before, on the back wards of psychiatric hospitals. Now the major difference was that I appeared to be one of them, rather than one of the staff.

I still knew absolutely nothing about my own diagnosis. I could only assume, from being in the presence of my fellow patients, that whatever I had, it was not good.

I am an anxious person under general conditions, and I have learned to consciously direct this anxiety in a variety of usually constructive ways. But now, by the time I was placed in my hospital bed, my hands were sweating, my heart was pounding, and my mind was racing furiously to devise ways of intellectually removing myself from this new reality. I had brought an enormous novel with me to the hospital and, picking it up and putting it down several times in each hour, I probably read close to four hundred pages during that afternoon and evening.

I never did understand any reason for being in that hospital on Saturday and Sunday. My neurologist was not on duty on the weekend. It was clear from the start that I would have to wait until Monday morning even for routine checks by the nurses, on the doctor's orders. I managed to sleep fitfully through the first night. The only positive memory I have of that night is that there was a black nurse who came to check on me occasionally. She was a friendly human being who treated *me* like one. Her touch of human kindness helped me get through that night. I was not so fortunate on some succeeding nights.

The details of the next day, Sunday, are not clear in my mind except that it was a boring, interminable length of time, mostly just waiting. My family's visit helped to while away time, which was no longer measured for me by a clock. Rather, time became a matter of one event related to another, or of filling lonely voids with some human contact or with my long-ago-learned escape into reading and intellectual introspection. I did ask for some type of sedative to sleep through Sunday night, and after much delay I was finally given a sleeping pill.

This was the end of phase one in my learning how to be a dying patient. Thus far I had learned simply how to be processed as a patient without any specific diagnosis. However, I was taught, particularly by the orthopedist and by the examination in the neurologist's office, that I was becoming a patient under some unspoken but dreadful conditions. Thus far, the nursing personnel on the ward treated me like any other patient. Presumably, this was because they had no medical information at that point which indicated why I was there. My presence on a ward with many patients who had been rendered speechless and virtually senseless by neurosurgery seemed as puzzling to the nurses as to me.

# CHAPTER TWO

# *Toward Diagnosis*

The second phase in my processing began on Monday. Perhaps it was signaled by some of the nurses trying to be a little funnier, using the tricks of their trade to cheer up the patient. Wanting to escape their ministrations, I spent part of Monday morning sitting in a reading room at one end of the ward. This did not prove to be much of an escape. The deteriorated patients, for whom neurosurgery had been a failure, were occasionally wheeled into this room and left there by the nurses.

One man in particular burns vividly in my memory. The grayish-black hair on his head was just beginning to grow back after his brain surgery. His vision seemed unimpaired, but that was about all that was not severed by the surgeon's knife. He growled and grumbled in an effort to communicate with other human beings. He was strapped into his wheelchair so that he could not harm himself or others. He had a large piece of old canvas cloth on his lap. Periodically he would grasp the canvas in his fumbling hands and shred a section of the cloth into small pieces. He seemed to attack the canvas with silent delight and with an intensity about his being. The expression of profound rage and impotence and insult, as he attacked it, struck me with a force that almost caused me to tremble in his presence. Even though the surgery had seemed to excise the soul of this man, some raw aspect of his humanity came through.

Was this what would happen to me? I could barely tolerate asking myself that question, and in fact, I really don't think I allowed myself consciously to consider that possibility. I did know that I could not tolerate the presence of

that man, and I fled back to my bed. Why could I not tolerate this man, when I had been so giving and so understanding of hundreds like him in a psychiatric hospital?
Now I was simply too vulnerable to try to deal with this,
and for my own temporary survival decided I would avoid
that kind of encounter again.

Sometime on Monday afternoon, the neurologist briefly
presented himself. He is a junior partner in a group that has
some national reputation based on research in conjunction
with a distinguished medical school. He introduced me to
three of his medical students and did a brief examination
in their presence.* From that point on, I saw much more of

---

* Editor's note: From "Notes of a Dying Professor," op. cit.,
about this neurological examination:

Again I got a reinforcement of the sense of not only am I
a patient who is supposed to behave in a certain way but
I'm almost an object to demonstrate to people that I'm not
really people any more, I'm something else. I'm a body that
has some very interesting characteristics about it, which include twitching of the muscles, rather symptomatic of this
particular disease.

And because it's a rare disease and not much is known
about it, it was very instructive for these medical students to
see these symptoms. But the point I want to make is that I
felt treated as an object. Being a patient is one thing, but
being an object is even less than being a patient. And I
began to feel not only the fear of this unknown, dread thing
that I have, that nobody knows anything about—and if they
know, they're not going to tell me—but an anger and a re-
sentment of "God damn it, I'm a human being and I want to
be treated like one!"

And feeling that if I expressed that anger, I could be
retaliated against, because I'm in a very vulnerable position.
One, nobody is going to tell me what the hell is wrong with
me, anyway. And two, if I do strike out, what's going to
happen to me as a consequence? So there is a sense of anger,
a sense of being terribly vulnerable—all of this setting in by
Monday.

the students than I did of the neurologist. Two of the students were husband and wife, which I found a delightful circumstance in this conservative and staid medical school. The third student, a male, remains rather foggy in my mind. I found myself able to communicate somewhat more easily with the woman student than with either man.

Monday afternoon I had an efficient programming, a series of tests and procedures to rule out a variety of diseases, narrowing down to a more precise diagnosis. Mundane procedures were started, such as routine blood tests from samples drawn every morning and every afternoon. My temperature and blood pressure were taken regularly, along with urine specimens. The grander and more painful examinations were yet to come.

The exact sequence of all these events now blends into a general memory of the entire trauma. However, my memory of each event is still very accurate. Perhaps it was Monday afternoon when a friend of mine who worked in the hospital came to visit me. It was an important visit, because he put me in touch with one of the staff social workers, who helped me to maintain my sanity in an insane world closing in on me.

My friend, the chief of the Social Service Department in the hospital, modestly suggested that he would make available to me one or more of his experienced social workers to discuss my medical situation anytime I wanted someone else to discuss this with. By Monday I wasn't ready for that; my wife and I had honestly dealt with this situation, as we had with many situations in the past twenty-one years. That relationship helped me through Monday, but by about Tuesday we both needed more than that.

It was on Tuesday when the neurologist brought the three medical students to my bedside to observe his neurological examination of me and to have them begin some of the preliminary examinations. I had the feeling that he might have been in a classroom lecturing to his students over a cadaver. Accustomed by now to his highly impersonal style, I was not upset by the lecture. I was, however, disturbed that he was inculcating into these students a dehumanization of the patient, and in particular, my own dehumanization.

By this time I was pretty good at anticipating the various types of neurological procedures and examinations, and I would promptly display the proper neurological response. Extensive X rays were ordered. One day was taken up with a spinal tap and another with an electromyogram.

During this time, my wife and I were trying to figure out exactly what the neurologist was trying to determine about the nature of my illness. What would these various examinations reveal? It was clearly not my prerogative to ask these questions or to receive any answers to them. I "had no right" to decide whether the procedures would be used, and I could not think how I might establish a right as a patient in relation to the physician and to the hospital.

I was so frightened by that time that I never really gave any serious thought to calling a halt to the procedures.

# CHAPTER THREE

# Grander Examinations

Arrangements were made for the three medical students to conduct the spinal tap. They were to extract spinal fluid for laboratory examination and also to conduct tests of the pressure of the spinal fluid along the spinal column. I had never had a spinal tap and I was very frightened of the procedures. I made a point of telling the woman student that it was important to this patient that he understand the procedures as much as possible. I wanted her to tell me as precisely as possible what to expect and what use would be made of this examination.

She was very clear and precise in describing the procedures to me, at the same time not going beyond this in giving me extraneous or unnecessarily worrisome information. She told me she wanted to go into pediatrics, and I said that I hoped she would learn from me that it was as important to adults as to children for them to understand what was happening to them. Being able to converse with her at some level of human contact was refreshing in itself. It also prepared me psychologically for this painful examination.

The major physical pain of the spinal tap was in the procedure for testing the spinal-fluid pressure. I do not recall the exact procedures but I do vividly recall the peculiar and exquisite type of pain accompanying it. It was as though someone had inflated a balloon within my spinal column to the point where the internal pressure simply could not be tolerated. It was unlike any other type of physical pain I had experienced.

I remember groaning and clenching my teeth, trying to

muffle my screams. I was very concerned that my pain would disturb and upset the other patients in the room. I finally managed to ask one of the medical students to give me a towel to bite on, so that I could muffle my screams. It occurred to me at the time that it was ridiculous to put a patient through this procedure in the immediate presence of other patients. Why in the world hadn't someone in this enormous institution considered not only my needs but those of my roommates as well? How unfeeling can human beings get toward one another? I felt certain that the last person who would consider these questions was the neurologist.

The examination was finally over, and I was physically and emotionally spent. I do remember telling the student that she had done a good job. She was responsive and kind throughout the exam, as were the other two students.

After this, I needed a social worker. I talked of my immediate concern for my family and my ability to face a terminal illness. That phrase, "terminal illness," in itself meant little to me except as it was put in terms of how long did I have to live. By this time it seemed very clear, in the face of all the evasiveness of all the people I had dealt with in the last week, that whatever I had, it would sooner or later take my life.

The social worker could neither confirm nor deny this. She told me that the spinal tap suggested a grave disease of some kind. And she allowed me to talk about my concern for my family and my fear of dying as well as to convey my rage and my shaken sense of myself. For two or three days, off and on, being able to talk with her helped me to survive the hospital ordeal.

Dying is a universal concern. It must come to the minds of many hospital patients. Then, why, among all the highly trained professional staff surrounding me twenty-four hours a day, was this one social worker the only human being, besides my wife, to whom I could really talk about it?

And what of all the other dying patients, who cannot find one social worker to talk to? My neurologist would probably consider this irrelevant and unnecessary to his determination of the proper medical care.

# CHAPTER FOUR

# Finishing at the Hospital

---

The final major examination was the electromyogram (EMG). I had never heard of this procedure before and had no basis for knowing what to expect this time. I could expect that I would be told very little about it, and that was correct. The examination consists of the insertion of long, thin, metal needles into major and minor muscles throughout the body. As the needle is inserted into the proper position in a muscle, an electric shock is produced to measure the response of that particular muscle. The response is transferred to an oscilloscope and recorded by closed-circuit television.

In essence, then, there is a written chart prepared on the response of each individual muscle tested. Apparently, the total examination, which takes two to three hours, provides a picture of the pattern and extent of muscle atrophy. It is a very painful procedure and much more prolonged than the spinal tap.

I was placed on a table in a special room with a technician who, trained by the medical staff, had become an expert in conducting this examination. She was a bright, cheery, and overly talkative woman who had graduated from high school only a few years before. She seemed particularly keen on conducting my examination in the presence of a visiting technician from a distant hospital. I thought I was witnessing a particularly vivid illustration of the psychological defenses that most technical people develop while working in hospitals. She is a good illustration of this, since she lacked some of the more sophisticated de-

fenses used by people with more education, such as physicians, nurses, etc. For all of her humor and banter, she
treated me essentially as a non-person throughout the painful examination. She discussed my body and the reactions of
my body during the examination as though these were not a
part of me. She had learned what was necessary for her to
learn in dealing with patients as patients. That is, she was
able to separate out any feeling and emotional response toward me in the examination, at the same time that she could
engage me in inane conversation.

Rather than upset her complete emotional compart-
mentalization, with possible negative consequences for me, I
played the game with her. Again, I was too vulnerable to do
otherwise. It was, however, demeaning and dehumanizing
to me to have to play this game with a postadolescent girl
who had an awful lot to learn about herself, let alone about
other people.

I think this girl understood enough of the nature and
seriousness of this procedure to know that it meant that I
had a grave illness. I wondered, during her banter, how far I
could go in playing this game with her. She joked about not
getting the needles in correctly sometimes. I said that if she
made a mistake and I died, I would see that the hospital
was sued. She laughed only halfheartedly at this, and I
seemed to have some small satisfaction in reaching the
limits of her total denial of the seriousness of my examination.

I knew that this would be the last major ordeal for me
at the hospital and that I would likely be discharged within
a day or so after the neurologist had the results of all the examinations. At the conclusion of this final EMG I really did
not care how negative or positive the results were. I simply
wanted to get out of that hospital. After that exam I was
exhausted in a way I had never known before. I was physically weak and remained so for several days.

Prior to that examination I was able to walk about the ward. My wife and I enjoy a drink before dinner and there was a delightful bar at the top of the hospital which has a very nice view of the metropolitan area. I got permission from one of the ward physicians to go to the bar. The first time, I put on my usual clothing and we were admitted. The second time, when the hospital ordeal was really getting to me, I did not put on my clothing but wore a very fancy bathrobe to the bar. I was not allowed to order a drink, because I was in patient's clothing.

This was a minor incident, but again it reinforced for me the treatment of myself as something quite different from a normal human being. Denied a cocktail with my wife, a small luxury to maintain some semblance of normality and of humanness, I silently raged at this treatment.

Starting about Wednesday, the neurologist indicated that he might have enough laboratory results to begin to give me some indication of the illness. Wednesday passed with no word from him. Thursday passed and he was still evasive. It was clear by this time that, whatever the illness, it was fatal. It seemed as though the neurologist could not face me with a diagnosis until he had somehow gone through a process necessary to him to conclusively establish, by exhaustive medical procedures, the fact that I was indeed dying.

On the day that I was to be discharged, Friday, the neurologist somehow screwed up his courage to discuss the findings with my wife and me. I had asked him from the start to be honest and straightforward with me. He did this with a literalness that left my wife in shock for some while to come. I was so emotionally numbed by this time that his almost brutal frankness did not carry the same overwhelming impact. He described in vivid, precise detail the nature of the continued atrophy of my muscles and how this would affect my various bodily functions. I was told that I might have as little as six months to live and maybe as much as three years.*

I left the hospital about noon on Friday and will never go there again. I was emotionally spent and physically weak to the point of needing my wife to support me as I walked. This was unrelated to my illness but a direct consequence of seven days of torture in a world-renowned hospital. It is a great medical research institution which pioneers the knowledge of many diseases. It also operates for a patient, such as myself, like a medieval, primitive place for controlling stigmatized patients and bending them to the will of well-

---

* Editor's note: In "Notes of a Dying Professor," op. cit., Archie tells the above part slightly differently:

By Friday the test results were all in. I knew that the major examinations had been completed. The main conference confrontation with the physician was about an hour before I was discharged. I had been in the hospital seven days. I was tired, irritable, angry—angry at the doctor, who was still being evasive. I had told him from the start that I wanted him to be open with me, that I wanted to know the full implications of whatever it was that I had. And up until the last hour I was there, it seemed to me that he could not face me with what he had to say.

He did then do essentially what I asked him to do, that is, to level with me regarding the diagnosis. It was a very hard thing for him to do. If he could have found any way of avoiding telling me, he would have. It was a terribly painful thing for him to have to lay it on the line. But he did. The way in which he did it was kind of staccato, impersonal, matter-of-fact. This is what the symptoms are, this is the progression of the symptoms. How long do I have to live? Six months to three years.

The only break in his façade was when I asked him to clarify. He had prepared a little speech. But any time I asked him for a little bit more information or a judgment on those facts, I could almost see his shell coming back.

meaning physicians, nurses, and other controllers of the lives of the patients imprisoned within its walls.

It was important for me to get back to work as soon as possible, since I was physically able to do that. I was very concerned about maintaining insurance and disability policies connected with my employment, and ashamed of how little I had planned for the financing of my family in the event of my death.

Where do you tell these fears and shames when you know you don't have long to live? I didn't know. I did not want or need a psychiatrist to tell my current troubles to. While the medical social worker's help was critical in the hospital, I did not need that now. My wife and I first tried to keep the fatal nature of my illness a secret, but then we realized we could not go on playing this kind of game for very long.

My first night home, I met with my children and wife and cried with them. I cried because I did not want to die, because I did not want to leave them. I was not and am not afraid of dying in itself, but at the age of forty-six, and wanting to see my children well established in life, I am not ready to die. My family, then, was the first to know of my shame and fears. Now I needed some other kind of help.

# CHAPTER FIVE

# *At Home*

My wife did not tell any of her friends or associates about my fatal illness, because I did not want my employers to know about it. I was still fearful that there would be economic consequences if it were known. My wife did single out one friend with whom we were able to talk. When I came home from the hospital, that friend and her husband were the first couple I saw who *knew*.

These friends brought a bottle of Swiss liqueur that they had been saving for some special occasion. We drank the delicious liqueur in my living room, acknowledging the fact of my dying and the necessity to plan in terms of the children and so on. The conversation as I recall it seemed trivial, but it was the first chance for my wife and me to talk openly with another couple about our unpleasant predicament. My friends were near tears throughout the meeting. I guess my wife and I were too, but tears had become rather commonplace for me. What seemed more important was the opportunity to openly express appropriate feelings and to carry on some human conversation.

I remember becoming very depressed and wanting to cry and sob in the hospital but being very concerned about upsetting the other patients. One evening at the hospital I stumbled into the bathroom and in the darkened silence I cried and sobbed against a cold, sterile bathroom wall. Now there was some restoration of my own dignity in being able to sit in my living room and confront other human beings with my own true feelings.

I was concerned at the time about placing an unfair

burden on my friends. Since then, I have come to see that other human beings, who don't know when they are going to die, also have to face their own feelings at some time.

The next person I wanted to talk to about my illness was a fellow professor who could perhaps give me some practical information about my financial situation as a university professor. He came to our living room, and when I told him what the doctor had told me, tears came to his eyes and it was very difficult for him to speak.

This friend did give me practical advice, some of which turned out later not to be so sound, but at that point it was very reassuring to me to be able to talk to someone else about my job and the implications of my illness. We agreed that my colleague's wife should not be told about my illness, because we all felt she could not handle it herself. This was the first of many decisions that we—my wife and I—made about various people's ability to handle their own feelings about my illness. We came to accept making these judgments.

At my request a third friend visited soon, a friend who had been trained as a social worker and was now in business. Since I had never been very astute about financial affairs, I wanted some sound business advice. When I told him I foresaw financial ruin for my family after my death, he insisted that I was not describing my core concern. In this he caught me off guard. I had expected him to concede that my family faced destitution, but in the face of his persistence I began to realize that what I was most concerned about was my guilt and shame. I had not provided what the family would need. I felt that I was a failure as a father, not just financially but totally.

In specifying this concern to my friend, I found a wellspring of emotion within me that had remained untapped throughout my ordeal in the hospital. The guilt and the long-built-up feeling of having been a less-than-adequate father burst out of me in a siege of crying and sobbing in front of my friend. He cried with me. Perhaps he cried *for* me, but he also cried *with* me in a way that helped me to begin to deal with my own feelings about dying.

He touched or stumbled upon another facet of my feelings: my children; and I could begin to move a little forward after that.

This friend, through a personal loan, enabled me to plan, right then and there, to ensure that my two older children could stay in college for the coming year. I had not been able to face that until this time, for I had been nearly immobilized. The amount of money at that time was really not so important, but knowing that I could definitely finance the children's education for another year was critical for me right then and there.*

---

* Editor's note: In "Notes of a Dying Professor," op. cit., Archie expanded upon the thoughts above:

Out of the hospital, there were other matters to consider. One was my dealings with my family. I don't think one ever deals with anything, with finality, in any one point in time, either with living or with death. I recall a Sunday New York *Times* review of a book by Robert Penn Warren. There was one quote from it: "The dream is a lie, the dreaming is true." Perhaps death is a lie and dying is true. The difference is between the nouns and the verbs. It's the "dealing" that is the truth, not the "deal."

. . . at any rate, I haven't "dealt with" my feelings about my family. I am constantly dealing with them, as I always have, but in a new and different context since my illness.

Although there are relatively few physically painful aspects of the illness at this stage, the psychologically painful aspect has certainly been my feelings about my family.

I have a son at college and a daughter at college and a ten-year-old boy† at home. And while I would like to see all my children well into adulthood, I find it particularly poign-

---

† Jimmy was really thirteen years old then. In calling him ten, Archie was disguising him in this anonymous article.

After this friend left, my wife recalled that he had said it was only money. And it *was* only money. But the loan meant that someone cared, appreciated, and understood

---

ant and difficult that I may not see my youngest child into adulthood. I feel a personal responsibility, and always have, for seeing that my children are on their own and psychologically and otherwise prepared to assume responsibility for themselves. And I certainly cannot expect a ten-year-old boy to be responsible for himself.

There are a variety of sources about why I feel very strongly in terms of my own family, which aren't terribly relevant here except that that was a strong part of my reaction, my depression, in the hospital. I never cry very much, but I certainly cried very profoundly, a depressive crying, in the hospital. And being self-analytical, I tried to ask myself what I was so depressed about.

At an intellectual level I could tell myself that I had some guilt feelings about my family, particularly about my children, and not deal with it very much beyond a kind of superficial recognition that it wasn't the illness or dying itself that was really bothering me but something more related to my relationship with my family and my feelings of not really having been as good a father as I should have been.

I was able to discuss some of this with the social worker while in the hospital, but I did not really come to terms with it then. . . .

After then telling of the conversation with the friend who helped him confront his guilt, he wrote further:

. . . it took some while, and particularly that friend, to get me to the point—and that was a critical point—of my feelings about my family, of really acknowledging to myself the guilt and inadequacy that I felt about my role as a father. If I hadn't arrived at that point then, I would have had to reach it sometime or else be overwhelmed by the guilt and the depression that comes from it.

And I've not been so depressed since then.

where I was at that point in time. And for a man who has made the collection of money important to himself, this was a most unusual act of giving from one human being to another.

Perhaps it should be mentioned that all the friends whom we turned to on my first weekend home from the hospital were Jews. I am not Jewish. These classifications are not very important to me, but I know they have all kinds of negative as well as positive implications to most people in this country. I mention it because these friends were critical to getting my wife and me back on the road leading to some semblance of a livable condition for whatever time we had together.

I was able to return to work the following day, to begin to face a new world of friends and professional associates from whom I felt I had to keep a secret about my illness. The main reason for the secret was a complicated financial one, regarding the newness of my employment.

Aside from the considerable burden for me in being this secretive, I had to learn to deal with other people's feelings about my illness. In some ways this was an extension of how I had to learn to adapt to the personnel in the hospital. Their attitudes toward dying are merely an extension of the larger societal attitudes toward dying. But I experienced this first in the hospital and then in the larger society.

I was strengthened and supported in preparation for this by the friends who came to our house and helped me begin to face the life I had left to live.

# CHAPTER SIX

## *Spring and Summer Events*

---

Many of my colleagues and students had sent kind cards and messages to me in the hospital. I was still visibly wobbly when I returned to work, and colleagues and students expressed sincere concern about how I was getting along and what had been wrong with me. I had developed a rather standard reply, depending upon how far the individual person went in questioning me.

It is a fascinating study in itself to analyze the way in which a person asks another about a serious illness. Some people ask rather innocuously, "Are you all right?" and let it go at that. Other people do not let it go and continue with questions until I refuse to answer them or indicate that their questioning is inappropriate. One rather clever line of questioning was asking me very directly if my illness was permanent. The answer I gave was, "Yes, it is permanent." This answer told that particular person what she wanted to know, and she was the only one of my colleagues to obtain that much information at that point.

The usual answer I gave was that they had not determined the diagnosis and would want to re-evaluate my condition sometime in June. This reply seemed to forestall further questioning on the part of most people. One student in one of my classes said that she was getting "bad vibrations" regarding my illness, and apparently she somehow picked up the severity of my illness. What was interesting to me was not only her perception of the seriousness but her unreadiness to handle her own feelings about it and wanting to let me know very clearly that she did not want any discussion of this.

I was able to continue all of my duties through the balance of the school semester with only one physical limitation, making a point occasionally of going home early for a nap or otherwise making certain that I did not overtax myself. I cut back a bit on the amount of individual conferencing I had with students but generally maintained my pretty full schedule at the University.

My wife and I had to make arrangements for housing for the next academic year, particularly in view of my illness and the uncertainty as to how long I could walk or drive to the University. We agreed to look for a house to rent near the University. The owner of one house which seemed acceptable to us was insisting that we sign a two-year lease. I did not want to commit my wife to so long a period for a house that might be unsatisfactory to her and my son after my death. I consulted with my wife, and we decided to level with the landlady, telling her that I had a terminal illness and did not want to rent for more than one year. The landlady agreed to this. She indicated that by coincidence her husband had died when her son was the age of my younger son. She had managed financially by buying a couple of homes and renting them. In any event, the landlady had an unusual appreciation for our plight, and we were glad to settle on her place to live for the next year.

It was midsummer when we gave up our midwestern home. The move from the old community, where we had lived for four years, was a very traumatic experience for me. Beyond the many practical complications, breaking the ties with our old friends was a particularly depressing and nostalgic time for me. I found that I could not face our friends who had brought the bottle of Swiss liqueur to our living room. I still don't know why I could not handle my feelings in that case. I was able to say my good-bys to other friends, though painfully. We moved, and left a great deal of love behind us.

Moving many miles away, to our new home, was the start of a new era or phase for us. In a very unplanned way, we used the summer to prepare ourselves for this new life. We visited a friend in New England, seeing that country for the first time. At times I used this vacation as an opportunity to begin to deal more directly with my own terminal illness.

I told our hostess about my illness, and she was able to discuss it with me to some degree. She was exceedingly kind and helped make our summer vacation a very nice one. However, she told my wife privately that she could simply not face the fact that I was dying. Given her feelings about this, her ability to relate to me in a very positive way raises questions about people who are much more conflicted about dying. What kind of personal torture or self-deception do they go through in being confronted by someone who is dying?

By the summer, some of my symptoms were increasing. In addition to my right hand, my left hand was becoming very weak. It was difficult for me to dress, particularly to use buttons. So my wife and I began to look for clothing, especially shirts, with zippers. We went to some New England resort stores. One elderly lady, operating a very fashionable men's clothing store, pressed me as to why I needed a zippered shirt. I answered that I had a serious disease which made it increasingly difficult for me to use buttons.

Since I appeared very healthy and able, this comment came as an obvious shock to this nice little old lady. Apparently feeling that she had to give me some kind of support, she asked me if I had gone to a doctor of osteopathy, because sometimes they can do a lot of good that regular doctors cannot do. I thanked her for the advice and told her that I had excellent medical advice and could live with the illness as I understand it.

My comment seemed to increase the anxiety and consternation of the lady, and I departed from her shop as quickly as I could.

A day or two later, I went to another clothing store in the same resort area and was waited on by a man I would judge to be in his sixties. Again I was queried as to why I had to have zippered shirts, and I gave the explanation regarding my handicap and illness. Again, this man would not settle for my initial explanation, and again I explained that I had an untreatable illness and simply had to begin to find clothing that I could use, in view of my physical limitations.

This encounter led the store man to say that he was going into Massachusetts General Hospital on the following day for surgery for possible cancer. It is rather bizarre, the way one runs into both illness and feelings about illness with other people. This man did not offer me any advice but tended to commiserate with me. He was obviously very much emotionally involved in his own situation, and our conversation came to a quick end.

We made arrangements for a new specialist to keep track of my illness in our new city. After a rather brief neurological examination he tended to confirm the findings of the other neurologist. He talked alone with my wife and then with the two of us together. My wife said that he told her he was appalled at the way in which the other neurologist had explained my illness and the length of time I might have to live. He also suggested to us that the elaborate and painful procedures I had in the hospital were really unnecessary to establish the diagnosis that was finally made. He felt that the diagnosis could have been made strictly on the basis of a clinical examination in an office.

In the face of that information, or at least that opinion, a lot of my feeling about the whole seven days in the hospital welled up over me. But with it all, I was gratified that this neurologist could handle his own feelings about the nature of my illness and that I could focus with him on whatever medical care I might need. He had been mentioned to me by a friend who described this neurologist as one of those who survived the German concentration camps. Whatever relevance that might have to his conduct as a physician, he was a refreshing and welcome contrast to my previous neurologist.

# CHAPTER SEVEN

## Reactions of Other People

I have tried to keep this account in some chronological order and maintain some perspective on the events. My intent is to try to convey beyond my own immediate, personal reactions the profound sense in which my reactions are determined by others around me. This is becoming increasingly difficult to maintain. In the past week, my symptoms have increased visibly, and I am becoming much more limited in what I can do. I see the early signs of my speech becoming affected, and I wonder how long I will be able to talk into this machine.* Nevertheless, I will try to continue with recounting some of the events.

By the time our vacation was over and we were settled in our new home, it was just about time for my fall-semester duties. Other faculty were returning, and I began to appear regularly at my university office. Up to this time, I had had few obvious physical symptoms. But now I was beginning to limp with my right leg. It was necessary to hold onto handrails and otherwise give some indication to an observer that there was, in fact, something wrong with me.

I vividly remember the response of a student who saw me limping across the lobby to my office. His eyebrows rose and his eyes widened, as his mouth fell open, staring with

---

* Editor's note: After several attempts to clarify the foregoing sentences, I decided to leave them about as originally recorded. Many thoughts are tumbling out together, important ones, perhaps harder to organize as he faced greater disability and dependence.

disbelief at my dragging leg. I thought at the time that perhaps this is the kind of reaction that I will soon find very
common.

I have seen a faculty member glance at me in the hall-
way and quickly turn away, as though to deny she had seen
me and recognized my disability.

This set of reactions to my physical condition is perhaps
similar to a black man inadvertently showing up at a D.A.R.
tea. It reminds me of the time, some twenty-five years ago,
that a date of mine, an attractive black woman, accompanied me to a posh opening of a show in Hollywood. The
glare of eyes upon us, and the unspoken comments, wrote a
story in themselves. One can quickly become accustomed to
this kind of silent perception by other people, but it becomes necessary for survival to remind oneself that it is
much more a commentary on others than it is on oneself.
That is, it is critical that one not take on or incorporate the
negative and stigmatized judgments of others in these situations.

Again I went through questioning by my colleagues,
similar to my experience when I returned from the hospital
in the spring. This time the critical point in the question and
answer seemed to be my friends' unwillingness to accept my
explanation of the permanent nature of my illness. It is as
though the rather sanitary word "permanent" enables one to
begin a gingerly approach to the fact of dying. Further,
since I work among a group of psychologically sophisticated
people, it was to be expected that many psychological interpretations would be made about my behavior and my illness.

One black friend who had had frequent contact with
me in the previous semester, seemed to have a strong need
to maintain his distance from me recently. Without attempting to interpret his point of view, I felt his frequent glances
at me suggested a sorrow and inability to confront with me

the obvious serious nature of my illness. I regret that we have not been able to continue our prior friendship.

One faculty member is teaching a course on death and dying. I told him why I had a very personal interest in that course. We discussed the possibility that I might appear before his class sometime during the semester. I discussed generally with him the reactions of other people to the visibility of my illness. He offered the opinion that only one faculty member could handle her own feelings and deal very directly with me regarding my illness. I was surprised at the individual he had singled out, since I would not have judged that person to be so liberated in her own thinking and behaving.

I started out each course this semester announcing to the students that I had a permanent muscle disease and that it would present some limitations on my physical activities. Generally the students have seemed to take this information very gravely, with a few students being able to deal much more directly with me than others. One black student in particular has a refreshing, honest approach to me in which he can verbally or non-verbally acknowledge my illness. Other students let it get in their way, to varying degrees, hesitating to approach me or apologizing for their demands upon my time.

I have tried to make a point of continuing to go to the Faculty Club for lunch, for social intercourse with my colleagues and others. Because my hands have become weakened, it is very difficult for me to handle the cafeteria-style lunch line. Through glances and gestures of my colleagues and not by words, it has been apparent that my physical condition has made itself increasingly evident to them. It is hard for me to light a match for a cigarette, and one colleague has taken it upon himself to be available to me for this service.

Another colleague with whom I have been close continues to encourage me in a number of mutual activities in which I can no longer take part because of my limitations. I tried to explain as gently as possible to him that my physical condition does not allow some of these activities. While I think he hears what I am saying, it seems as though he simply cannot face or accept the fact that I am no longer able to do many of these things.

I must look to myself and examine the clarity of my communications with my colleagues and others. That is, it is quite possible that my own conflicts about my illness somehow reflect themselves through the way in which I communicate my illness to these people. However, I am most certain that the problem in communication is much more with my colleagues and others than it is within myself. This is not to assess blame but to indicate the profundity with which an ill and dying person must take the burden of trying to communicate to others. And when this communication does not work, the dying person has the additional burden of helping the other person with his reactions. This is an unfair burden for me and any other dying person, yet if one is to try to stay in touch, it does become necessary for the dying person to take the initiative to assume responsibility, in order to maintain the contact.

Another phase or era of my life began a few weeks ago, when I purchased a cane. I had fallen at home a couple of times and it was apparent that I had better have some kind of support when my muscles suddenly gave out. The purchase of the cane symbolized a rather grim fact of my life at that point. Somehow I did not want to acknowledge that I needed a cane, and yet I could not deny the necessity for it. I went with my wife to a store that sold a variety of medical appliances and had a wide range of canes displayed before me. As I walked out of that store with the cane, it became a new, visible symbol of my illness.

I think that the first time I "appeared in public" with my cane was on a weekend meeting with a student and another instructor at the student's home. The cane was a necessity in order to manage the long stairway to the student's apartment. This particular student was somewhat surprised at the cane but certainly seemed able to deal with the reality of my need for it. This student has several years of working with ill people. His area of study will be the delivery of health services. I found myself hoping that he might find ways of delivering medical and other services to people like me in a fashion that might somehow remove the unnecessary barriers put there for us.

The next major appearance with the cane occurred at a student-faculty party one evening. My wife agreed that there seemed to be a stunned and silent reaction to my cane. The only exception was a colleague whom I had told some while before about my illness, who seemed to deny its existence. He kept inquiring about why I needed the cane. He has an unusual capacity for shutting out events and information he doesn't want to hear. However, I think my cane finally did get through to him.

It is at once silly and sad that my cane becomes a vehicle for communicating with some people, where communication would otherwise be impossible.

# CHAPTER EIGHT

# What Is Help?

Aware of my increased disability in the past few weeks, I have been more and more anxious to make available in one place all the medical care that I need, now and in the future. Since the University Hospital is only one block from my office, that seems the best location for all medical and physical therapy. To arrange this has meant going through the formal referral procedure again, from one physician to another and so on.

I asked the advice of a friend, a psychiatrist, about the quality of care at this hospital. He wanted to know my diagnosis and I told him, amyotrophic lateral sclerosis. His immediate response was that the diagnosis may not be certain and that this disease sometimes appears very similar to other diseases. I somehow did not expect this psychiatrist to have to avoid for his own reasons the unpleasant nature of my illness. I simply wanted his opinion about the kind of care I might receive. He was very kind in offering to ensure that I got referred to the proper places at the hospital, but he was playing games with himself and me.

Making these arrangements for my medical care at the hospital is one of many ways of preparing for my death. As unpleasant as it may seem, one of the ways in which I can preserve some sense of my own worth and dignity is to assume responsibility for preparing for my own dying and death. Somehow I cannot allow others to deny me at least this effort in my life.

～～～

Earlier, I have tried to present how it feels to be known as a person with a serious illness, whether or not it is known that one is dying. I have tried to describe how important the reactions of others become in defining one's own psychological and social realities. A great deal of academic literature has been written on this; Erving Goffman's books contain fairly accurate descriptions of the impact of others upon me in recent months.

However, this is only one side of the picture, and there is at least one other side: what it is like *within* myself, to know that I am dying, to be in the process of dying.

First, I will attempt to convey the nature of the illness. Thus far, there has been little or no physical pain involved in the steady advance of physical symptoms. An early symptom, some months ago, was the twitching of muscles to a point where they were annoying and frightening but not particularly painful. Most of that twitching has subsided, leaving me with visible deterioration and atrophy of muscles in my hands and arms. Thus, there is an obvious physical process that has been taking place in my body, of the body dying, as it were, in one part at a time.

The disease does not affect my brain, so that aside from my psychological reactions there is no mental or psychiatric impairment that necessarily accompanies this particular disease.

Psychologically, then, in contrast to the initial impact and assault upon me of my disease during and just after the hospital experience, most of my recent reactions seem rather small. I have had periods of depression, related, I am sure, to the anger and rage I feel about the irrevocable nature of my fate. These depressions, however, have not been long-lasting, and they have not occurred with as much frequency as I had expected.

One of my paramount concerns is that I not become a human vegetable, that is, hospitalized with virtually no senses remaining but kept alive interminably in a bed. I don't know what control I can have over this.

For the immediate situation, I try to keep up a variety of activities and contacts, within my limits, and this is my life.

Psychological preparation for dying does not seem to me very different from psychological preparation for living. I suppose that if I wanted to sit back and die tomorrow, I could to some degree increase the totally disabling pace of my illness. On the contrary, I want to enjoy what life I do have left and to live it in whatever manner I can. So dying, for me, is not, or at least should not be, separate from the efforts to engage myself in the life that I have at hand from day to day.

As I record my psychological reactions, I am apprehensive that they will be interpreted by some in purely psychopathological terms. I mention this not to argue against the need for psychological therapies and theories but to stress that there are many critical assumptions made in most psychological approaches that, to some degree, predetermine the way in which the individual is understood and treated. The popularization of psychological theories in this country has been accompanied by a tendency to interpret behavior and to do so irresponsibly. For example, the interpretation of "Freudian slips" has become a parlor game even among young children. This not only corrupts psychological theory and practice; it tends to become a destructive game between and among human beings.

I recently wrote a book review on William Ryan's book *Blaming the Victim*. Ryan, a clinical psychologist, tried to come to terms with his own psychological biases. Although I criticize the book on other grounds, I think he does provide a good illustration of the pathological bias of the helping professions and of psychological theories.*

To be more specific to my case, if society defines dying as abnormal, stigmatized, pathological, or worse, how can the dying individual escape the pervasive implications of these labels? How can you, my reader, view my psychological reactions without adding your own psychological interpretations? I don't think you can.

And can I myself escape them?

I hope that this record will assist both you and me by modifying the pathological implications of dying in our minds and hearts.

To my mind, dictating this book serves two purposes: First, it may be helpful to others to read of my experience, particularly since I tell it within the context of the understanding of human beings that I have consciously developed for professional reasons. Second, working on it serves some therapeutic purpose for me. It is not unlike the accounts of some Jewish prisoners in German concentration camps who studiously analyzed the camps and their fellow prisoners. Bruno Bettelheim, perhaps the best-known recorder of horror in a concentration camp, felt that his work preserved his own sanity in the camp. Victor Frankl, the Austrian existential psychoanalyst, recounted a similar autobiography, originally titled *From Death Camp to Existentialism*. These and other accounts strongly indicate that the will to survive,

---

* Editor's note: Ryan develops another argument that has bearing here. He points out that many success-oriented writers and opinion makers in our society put down as "losers" those who have not had society's benefits. Technical, scientific labels and phrases can also become vehicles for carrying on this attack, which goes on virtually unchallenged since the victims seldom are in a position to defend themselves. (William Ryan, *Blaming the Victim* [New York: Pantheon, 1971])

combined with specific measures to counteract the insanity of one's environment or situation, can have some mitigating effect. While this was not my sole purpose in writing this book, I certainly had these studies in mind when I began it.

I have finished playing games with others on the subject of my illness and my dying. In refusing, I may come across as hostile; in fact, I probably did recently with the neurologist; but I will not forfeit my own well-being while he or anybody else plays out a role. Virtually nothing is known medically about my disease; there is no treatment for it; my body tells me more accurately about symptoms than any physician can tell at this point. While I do not deny that the skill and technical knowledge of the physician are invaluable in many situations, in some, in my own, his role is a very limited one, and I do not intend to aggrandize it.

Our society rewards medical practitioners entirely out of proportion to their specific value in the society. While I am not about to take on the challenge of reforming the medical profession, neither will I spend the remainder of my life meeting the emotional demands of its practitioners. To be more specific, in the past week I had this examination by a neurologist as part of my plan to have all of my medical care located in one place. The midwestern neurologist was supposed to forward my records from last spring for this new examination, but they did not arrive. The new neurologist had to rely upon my own statements and upon his clinical examination. While he accepted my statement of the initial diagnosis, he seemed very uncertain about my understanding of the full implications of it. When I demonstrated my understanding, he seemed to let down his mask of impersonal professionalism. It was as though he was relieved of having to keep secrets from me. On the other hand, he seemed to allow himself to express some of the depression he felt about the gravity of the illness. I said in my perhaps cryptic and hostile manner that I did not want to play games and I did want to be very clear about the various stages of my illness and the care that would be necessary.

He told me that he has a patient, a housewife in New Jersey, who has ALS but does not know it. I fixed my eyes hard upon his and asked if he were really sure that she did not know. He avoided my gaze. I said that there were many ways of communicating information to patients, and that I would be very doubtful if she did not have some sense of the seriousness of her illness. I added that it was very difficult, if not impossible, to determine in some situations whether knowledge of the illness was more painful for the patient or for the physician. The neurologist mumbled agreement. Then I added that there were some patients who were too psychologically vulnerable to handle the fact of death, but there were many more who could handle it.

As I write about it, what I am trying to suggest is that physicians are not in any special position to help with the problems of the dying patient. On the contrary, some, out of their own conflicts, complicate the lives of those patients. Perhaps this seems to say only that physicians are more human than otherwise. However, it is also to say that if the dying patient really wants help at this critical moment in his life, he must turn elsewhere. I turned to social workers, and I got some of the help I needed.

After returning here from the hospital last spring, I continued confronting my illness and dying in sessions with a social worker. We met once a week for about three months. I remember discussing the guilt about what kind of father I am (becoming a cripple and so on) for a thirteen-year-old boy, and wouldn't it really be better for me to think in terms of not being in the family, whatever that might mean? Perhaps I should make some other plans for myself? What can I really contribute to my son by being in the home? Very quickly, with the social worker, I decided that that's a lot of baloney, and that I can play a role, an important role, for him and for me, regardless of what physical shape I'm in. I came to understand better some of my conflicts with the family, which I had tended to confuse as I reacted to the fact of dying. In spite of my bravado and intellectual understanding, I also found in corners of my mind a wish to run away from my illness. I began to learn to live one month, one week, one day at a time.

There is nothing magical or even very complicated or profound in this kind of help. There is, however, some reaffirmation of my own humanity in it. Unfortunately, few dying people know about or have available to them any kind of help in looking at their individual fears and concerns. They may know only that their lives are governed by the physicians and nurses in immediate attendance.

I get along without a social worker at present. But I rely upon the knowledge that one will be there as I need one in the course of my dying.

# CHAPTER NINE

# The Importance of Functioning

Of increasing importance to me is the help of occupational therapists, who can provide me with a variety of aids and appliances to keep me physically mobile. Simple, practical help becomes of enormous importance in maintaining some degree of my daily functioning. My first O.T., a man with a direct and kind manner, provided me with a buttonhook, so I could button and unbutton my clothing. I had an almost childlike, happy response to discovering this little tool. I now have a second occupational therapist, and she, too, is oriented toward the practical, day-to-day assistance I need in maintaining myself. There is no "tea and sympathy," but direct and straightforward, practical help.

I could not help questioning their indoctrination in one respect. Both seemed inbued with a principle that the patient must initiate the request or indication for a particular kind of device or aid. That is, the patient would not be encouraged to use devices that he himself does not yet see the need for. I suppose this principle may be generally sound, but I can imagine times for overruling it.

In any event, I am most grateful for the collection of gadgets that I have to keep myself going. With some of these fancy devices lodged in our kitchen, visitors are going to imagine that a great French chef must be in residence. My wife is a good cook; a French chef she is not.

It becomes more and more difficult to maintain my professional work life in the face of my constant need to be supported by my family. For instance, we were recently considering a trip to California to visit relatives. I did not feel I could enjoy the trip, but I did want Mary and Jim to go. Mary did not want to leave me home for three or four days even if someone were to look in on me. I thought that could be considered, and I did not want my needs to interfere with the plan.

This is only one of many examples of how my dependence impinges on others and leaves me with conflict. In the course of it I find it very hard to separate out what is the reality of my illness and what my reaction to it, as well as what is my need and what the need of the others.

They, too, have their conflicts. Fortunately they can verbalize them.

Throughout the past few months it has become increasingly evident to me that my own sanity and well-being depend upon my ability to continue in some kind of work; my sense of self-worth and dignity are tied up with it; that is, as long as I can continue to function as a professor, my life has specific meaning for me. Without denying the importance of family and family affairs in my value system, I still would find the alternative of staying home or of giving up my work to be a real ending of my life as I have known it. Though long a critic of the work ethic, I can see that I have allowed work to become such a central part of my life that I simply have to keep at it as long as I can. To me, that fact demonstrates the measure of work in society's ethos.

During the summer, I abandoned some of my scholarly writing and decided to give some priority to the narrative recounted here. The balance of my time and energy goes into preparation for and involvement with my students. However, interminable faculty meetings seem to cut into this time constantly.

I do not know how to prepare myself for the days when I can no longer perform my work role. I think about somehow extending the time during which I can perform adequately as a professor and classroom instructor. In any such adjustment, my colleagues will have a considerable degree of influence. Generally a kind and understanding group of professional educators, still they are in the midst of severe turmoil and concern about the future direction of their educational efforts. Thus, I will be engaged in a struggle for remaining in my teaching position at a time when the general environment of my department is one of extreme tension and conflict. While this does not change the nature of my activities and participation at the moment, I do have a sense of vulnerability in this climate as my handicap increases. Self-doubt can so easily grow as others raise questions, though perhaps covertly, if one's handicaps are inescapable.

I am sure that at some point some of my colleagues must ask themselves whether my illness has a negative impact upon students. While I think that question may often be generated by the faculty person's own ambivalence about illness and dying, at times I cannot avoid asking myself the same question.

So far, I think I can demonstrate to my own satisfaction that I can and do offer something of value to my students. Except for classroom instruction, I do not know, however, what educational role I can justify as the central basis for my continued employment. I am planning to explore alternatives at the University. Even as I pursue these possibilities, however, I am doubtful and conflicted about what I have to offer. I would like to think that I could make some contribution of longer-range impact than my day-to-day teaching. I remember once writing in a paper that every man wants to leave his mark. Perhaps this is my own small struggle for some form of immortality.

Whereas this account is motivated by much more pragmatic concerns, such as money, I hope that I will also be able to find ways of taking part in meaningful educational reform. It would be a nice luxury to know that I had taken part in developing some new studies in my area of expertise. This would require that I become involved in larger political processes, and I am very uncertain how much time and energy I have for that. I would be willing to devote the rest of my life to such an effort, however, and in the next few weeks I will try to explore what alternatives, if any, may be open to me.

I suppose there is an urgency, among many dying people, to crowd into that unknown, remaining period all the things they never did, all the things they thought they might do someday. That has not been especially the case for me. I have previously done a lot of the things I have wanted to do. In this way I have been more fortunate than most people. (For instance, when Mary and I were first married and finishing college, we took off without any money and spent a year in Mexico. There weren't very many people of our generation who just "took off" into the wilds. But we did, and we had a fabulous year working on a UNESCO project.) And I have assumed that in the next five or ten years I would simply build upon that past.

Now I do not have five or ten years, and it is a matter of trying to decide what I can do and what priorities I will assign for the balance of my life.

# CHAPTER TEN

## *New Frights*

A week has passed since I last recorded this narrative. In that week my disabilities have increased. There are some mild symptoms that my throat muscles are continuing to atrophy. This is very frightening, because I rely upon speech as a last means for communicating and remaining active.

Seating myself at the dinner table last night, I stumbled and fell to the floor. This is the first time I have fallen since I started using a cane, several weeks ago. Although I bore only a minor skin bruise, falling to the floor was a most frightening and helpless experience for me. I am sure it must have scared Mary and Jimmy even more. I remained on the floor for a few minutes before attempting to get up, to be sure that I had no serious injury. Lying there, immobile and feeling beaten by the unseen force of my illness, there was a fleeting moment of wanting to give up completely right then and there. But I fought that feeling immediately and gradually struggled within myself to begin over again.

It is as though each one of these incidents is a personal kind of defeat, and each requires a very personal kind of struggle, like going back into a boxing ring to be knocked down again.

# CHAPTER ELEVEN

# Death:
## A Psycho-Social-Ethical Problem

I have recently read a book on death and dying written by a psychiatrist named Elisabeth Kübler-Ross. The book was loaned to me in preparation for my participation in an interdisciplinary seminar on death and dying. The book grew out of the author's experience with dying patients. I volunteered to participate in the seminar, describing my own situation and my reactions to it. I hope that the seminar, conducted by a colleague of mine, will be tape-recorded and that it can be included in this narrative.

Out of her learning from the patients, Kübler-Ross has postulated five stages of dying: denial and isolation, followed by anger, bargaining, depression, and acceptance. Presumably, these categories emerge from the attempt to make order out of the psychological processes she observes most dying patients go through.*

While I have no major arguments with the book, and I assume it makes an important contribution to professional understanding, I would somewhat resent being locked into one stage or the other at any point of my dying. As in much psychiatric and psychological theory, categories tend to pigeonhole the patient and to predetermine the responses of professionals and others on the basis of that pigeonholing.

---

* Editor's note: Dr. Kübler-Ross has become recognized as perhaps the foremost contemporary authority on the psychological needs of dying patients. See her several books, especially *On Death and Dying* (New York: Macmillan, 1969).

After reading the book, I can see that the social worker at the midwestern hospital was applying Kübler-Ross's theories as she worked with me. For example, the implied "ideal" stage for a patient is that of acceptance. Just before my discharge from the hospital, the social worker commented that she had known very few dying patients who had moved "to acceptance" so quickly. I thought of the comment as a puzzling but complimentary observation by the social worker. I now feel that she very much had in mind the stages described in that book.

I think I do accept my dying, but it is not a single or unitary stage in itself, at least for me. And I doubt that "acceptance" is an unqualified stage for any dying patient. Fear and ambivalence recur time and again, as does depression. Psychoanalytically, depression is to some degree the consequence of repressing anger. To order these two reactions as separate and sequential stages is not entirely logical.

Quite aside from the neatness of the psychological theory, the patient must be seen in terms of wherever he is, at that time. One of the dysfunctions of these stages is that they may do a great injustice to the multiple feelings a patient may be having at any one time.†

---

† Editor's note: At the seminar in December 1971, a month or two after this part of the diary was recorded, Archie made these observations about Kübler-Ross's formulations:

. . . there are various levels of acceptance. Life for me is today, and I might accept some things today and not accept them tomorrow. I may get very angry, but I'm not likely to get depressed. I think most depression is related to unconscious anger, if you'll pardon my psychoanalytic bias. Many depressed people are seething with anger. It's their inability to deal with their anger that is often behind their depression.

I've seen this clinically in people that I've worked with, and I've seen it in myself. I may get depressed, but if I do, I'll stop and ask myself what I am angry about, and the

As a matter of fact, Kübler-Ross does not seem to allow her categorization to interfere with her more spontaneous and profound sense of being with the patient on his own

---

depression is very likely to go away. . . . In the hospital, I was concerned whether I would be able to use self-analysis and manage to control the depression. I asked one of the doctors about antidepressants. But I haven't used any drugs for that.

"Negotiating" makes sense as a stage. I think we all negotiate to some degree as long as we're living. I can't see how you can be in touch with any other human beings and not do some negotiating, maybe not specifically in the way Kübler-Ross means it in the dying patient. But I don't see that as a completely separate thing from "acceptance." These are the kind of analytical, classifying schemes that good scientists may try to formulate when knowledge is very limited. And we're at an early stage of knowledge about death and dying.

But the classificatory system can be reified, too. It can be treated as though those categories are imperatives for all people. One of my grave concerns about psychiatry—psychoanalysis in particular—is that the theory has moved way beyond the empirical realities, that we have developed a theory, and the diagnostic categories are in fact very questionable. It's an important development of knowledge about psychology, but we can overvalue that knowledge in a particular diagnostic classification and do great injustice to many people by imposing knowledge that really is not that well grounded.

I have worked with a lot of schizophrenic patients, and there is as much variation among people diagnosed as schizophrenic as there is among people diagnosed as psychoneurotic. So what does the diagnosis "schizophrenia" mean? I'm not saying it doesn't have utility, just as I'm not saying that Kübler-Ross's five stages don't have utility. But I am saying that to make universal application of those concepts to all people who are dying does a grave injustice to some people.

terms. And I am inclined to think that it is there, on our ability to be human beings with one another, that we helping people should place our emphasis, rather than on being faithful and locked into our professional postulates and biases.

One of the cases cited by her is that of a man in the final stages of ALS, the disease I have. Describing himself as "dead up to the head," the patient illustrates a number of the dilemmas of a dying patient and the professionals who surround him. It brings home to me my strong, recurring need to deny or wipe out the final stages of my illness, particularly the possibility that there might be a prolonged series of efforts to keep me alive in a very limited sense of that word.

Aside from the unpleasantness of having to live through those final days, weeks, or months, I am really appalled at the costs of hospital and medical care prior to my death. I have not made any adequate financial arrangements for my family in terms of dying. The prospect of having a few small life-insurance policies wiped out by medical bills prior to my death is grim and very difficult for me to accept. The cost of dying with my illness seems so unreasonable and unfair, especially to my children and my wife. It obviously reactivates some of my conflict about not being an adequate provider for my family, but on another level it simply reflects an insane system of not providing health services to the middle class as well as to the poor.

I am not sure how far Congress's proposed health-care legislation will get us in terms of more humane care of sick and dying people, but certainly situations such as mine are causing some physicians, hospital administrators, and others to seriously question their own ethics as they are involved in the current financial system of health services. We have yet to match the rhetoric about our Great Society with actual practices toward the weak, the dying, and the disadvantaged. I expect that I will fare much better than most in my situation, and yet even my future includes the distinct possibility of exhausting my meager resources by the time of my death.

Mrs. Rose Kennedy once commented in regard to the assassination of two of her sons that there was something very "unnatural" about a parent burying her children. The comment struck me as very poignant at the time. Now it takes on new and additional meaning for me. It does not seem "natural" to die before old age. While I do not belabor the question of why this happens to me, I do not "naturally" accept it either.

I have two children just starting college and a thirteen-year-old boy, and I had expected to be able to see my own children matured, perhaps producing my grandchildren. It is unnatural to be denied this. So I will go to my death accepting death as part of living but not at all accepting some of the circumstances surrounding it. And this, I think, is a vital distinction. We do not need to accept or tolerate the many implications of the exorbitant cost of dying borne by the families who survive. We do not need to accept or tolerate the imperious authority of professionals in absolute control over the dying patient. Increased psychological understanding of the patient must not be a substitute for an equally necessary scrutiny of the system of caring for patients.

My one effort at consistency in this account is to repeat and repeat the interconnection and inseparability of the psychological and the broader social implications of dying in our society. To focus on only one or the other is to miss the whole point. To deal with psychological and social aspects simultaneously is difficult, if for no other reason than that it tends to force a confrontation with the profound underlying moral and ethical issues we strive desperately to avoid.

This is the case when the physician cannot deal with his own feelings about death and his dying patient. But that is only "the tip of the iceberg." A physician in this country generally practices in a financial system that has little or no moral justification. A recent conference on medical ethics in Boston, I believe sponsored by a Kennedy foundation, sounds as though a Pandora's box of moral dilemmas and contradictions is just barely being examined. The impact of medical technology, which is the direct product of practicing physicians in this country, has enormous implications for the meaning and definition of life and death. Technology may be able to keep me alive for months or years, but who makes that decision? And what are my rights, if any, in that decision?

There are, I am sure, many little decisions along the way which will have to be made. Who will make them? How much will I be involved? How much will be left to my wife to decide? How much will physicians and others avoid these decisions, with the net effect of leaving the burdensome moral decisions basically in the hands of my wife. And why are my moral judgments not as valid as anyone else's?

As a nation, we pride ourselves upon being a very moral people, incorporating a pluralistic set of moral and ethical principles. We frequently speak of our Judaeo-Christian heritage. At an abstract and general level, these principles hold up well. At a concrete and specific level, we violate them constantly. Hiding behind professionalism is perhaps one of our favored ways of masking the inherent moral dilemmas in much of what we do.

I think this can be illustrated by my recent experience in the occupational-therapy department. I was waiting for a small appliance to be made for me when a young black man was wheeled into the room for an arm cast to be made. There was a kind of perfunctory reception of this young man in his wheelchair. He looked confused and apprehensive, and no one seemed to respond to this. There was some scurrying around to be sure that a physician had made the proper referral and to determine the details of the type of arm cast that should be made.

The patient and I were left to sit near one another while this activity was going on in the background. When I asked him about his injury, he said that he had been shot in the arm and the bullet had been surgically removed on the previous day. He was very concerned about recovering the full use of his right arm, but no one had told him anything about the nature of his injury or possible recovery. He conveyed to me, in a very few minutes, his concern and fear in the face of ambiguous information, or no information at all, from the people who surrounded him in the hospital.

I was treated with consideration and respect that contrasted with what was shown him. Whatever caused the distance between him and the staff, whether racial or social, or both, I felt it was marked. Although a great deal was being communicated to him wordlessly, no one was trying to find out what he might have wanted to communicate.

So seldom do we seem to see the dehumanizing effect of avoiding realities with one another!

Moral judgments are made in our everyday behavior as they were in the behavior toward this young man. Moral judgments are made non-verbally toward me in the everyday reactions of those around me. Somehow these must be brought out into the open, and they will require more than psychological understanding or interpretation on the part of professionals.

I have a few more arrows to shoot at the general target of psychological theory. Take my own idealism and impatience, shown in the story of the young black man, above. Psychology teaches that idealism and impatience may be engendered in early childhood and in adolescent fantasies. I can see this as I review some of my childhood conflicts. Also, I can see that, since organized religion serves no personal purpose for me, my own sense of idealism and morality is important and stands on its own ground, apart from psychological interpretations. Further, my illness is requiring me to learn in my middle age some sense of patience. Putting on my shoes and putting on my pants are new learning experiences in themselves. But my sense of injustice and outrage at what happens to many of my fellow men, and now to me, must be accounted for by more than a psychological explanation of the source of my impatient idealism.

I am dying, and you, the reader, are diminished to the extent that my dying is inhumane. We are all diminished by inhumane acts.

I do not expect the world to change tomorrow. And as much as I was moved by Martin Luther King, I do not subscribe to his epitaph of seeking release and freedom in death. We free ourselves and make ourselves human in the here and now, not in the hereafter. And I do not see that kind of liberation occurring solely through a preoccupation with one's own psychological self. I know a psychologist of my age who has spent his life trying to find himself through various forms of psychological therapy and group psychological experiences. He is not free, and I do not think he will ever find his freedom this way.

My brand of idealism, then, is not a personal quest for Nirvana. Perhaps, however, it is to be defined partly in the context of a highly sensitized awareness of John Donne's injunction: "Send not to know for whom the bell tolls, it tolls for thee." If we really believed and acted upon the belief that no man is an island, perhaps we would begin to evolve social relationships and a social order that would enable us to confirm our humanity to one another through our daily acts.

This is my brand of idealism. I know that we are a long way from achieving it. I know that my own life manifests many contradictions in the face of this ideal. At the same time, I have tried to live it as well as I can. And there is some small gratification in knowing for myself that I have tried. I will continue trying, to the end.

# CHAPTER TWELVE

## An Ethnic Fantasy

I have ruminated or fantasied about what kind of memorial service I might desire as some recognition of my life and death. In considering such a service from time to time, I have wondered what might bring together the wide variety of friends I have had over the past many years. Many friends, scattered from California to the East Coast, are Jews and blacks. Many of these people have little in common, and perhaps some would not speak to one another.

I really have no ethnic or religious identity of any importance to me. My own worth as a human being really does not require such an identification. At the same time, I know that for many of my friends some such identification is a necessity.

I don't know what would bring together these diverse groups of great human beings. Certainly my death will not. But it is fun to fantasy that a small group of black jazz musicians, along with a Jewish cantor, and some great black religious singing, with kosher wine flowing freely, might produce a very happy time.

But this is my own personal fantasy and not social reality.*

Prior to my marriage, I lived off and on and very frequently with a black family in southern California, and I

---

* Editor's note: I think Archie wanted his friends to actually celebrate his dying, and he thought that in the process they might enjoy exploiting and laughing at some of the stereotypes of their groups. As it happened, his family arranged a memorial service that carried out his fantasy to a remarkable degree.

was often the only white person in a variety of black social activities. I absorbed black culture, especially modern jazz, and that has been an important part of my own cultural life. Walking around in my white skin, I believe I can see and feel things about the black experience that many white people are denied and that some black people would want to deny me.

The year that my wife and I spent in rural Mexico not only was another major life experience that diluted the importance of ethnic and religious identification but also washed out my sense of nationalism. Working and living in some of the most "primitive" villages in the world, I came to appreciate the profound sense of human relationships that perhaps only isolated village people can have. I returned from that year in Mexico with very little false pride in American technology and values.

My earlier interracial and interreligious social life has been reinforced to some degree during my more recent years in the Midwest and on the East Coast. I will never quite adjust to the intense ethnic identification of peoples in the Midwest and on the East Coast, in contrast with my life in northern California. In St. Louis or Philadelphia, for example, if one is not a Jew or a Catholic or a Protestant or a black, what is one? Apparently not very much, in terms of one's psychological and social identity.

I have been particularly fascinated in recent years with the intricate business of Jewish identity. I think that many black intellectuals have borrowed, to some degree, from this developing notion of Jewish identity in the United States. Considering some of the confusion and dilemma it has created for American Jews, I certainly have some reservation about American blacks borrowing uncritically from this tradition.

Apart from that reservation, the more I have been exposed to the range of Jewish identities, the more it seems that a great and pleasant myth is perpetuated by a people.

If this offends some of my Jewish friends, no offense is intended. However, as you reserve the right to define me as a "goy," I reserve the right to exercise some critical faculty on your Jewish identity. One of my dear Jewish friends has gone so far as to label me as a "house goy." This is a clever combination of "house nigger" and "shabbes goy." It has some hostile overtones, but it nevertheless is affectionate and funny. And I have come to have a special appreciation for Jewish humor, which is a mixture of the intolerably sad with hostility and humor all rolled up into one.

And it is, as a black friend recently told me, that you laugh sometimes when it hurts so much that you want to cry. This is the profound human experience that blacks and Jews share with each other, and so few of them recognize or want to admit it.

I was called "Whitey" when I was five or six years old, because my skin was so white and my blond hair was almost white during the summer. Although this nickname vanished as I went into adulthood, I always thought of that term with some fondness. Since "Whitey" has taken on very different connotations in recent years, it is my private joke to recall it as my label.

I am glad to have known so many people from many different backgrounds and to have had my life enriched by their diversity. Perhaps that is a small glimpse of what is yet to come in our society, but I am sure there will be many struggles before this occurs on any large scale.

I have looked forward to witnessing how my children would find their own unique sense of adult identity and of purpose in their lives. Thus far, it has not been any easier for them than for me. But I have a hope and excitement that as their lives evolve they will find ways of relating and involving themselves with a variety of human beings well beyond what I have found. And I really had hoped to vicariously enjoy their discoveries. I will not have that opportunity now.

I especially hoped to see, at first hand, another generation come along, that is, my grandchildren. This was not a desire for self-perpetuation through parenthood but, rather, a curiosity and anticipation of what the world would begin to look like for yet another generation. I guess my idealism and enthusiasm lead me to think that my children's children will be making and living in a world something like the one I have hoped we might have had earlier.

I do have some regrets, and this is one of them.

# CHAPTER THIRTEEN

# Fighting for Life—Why?

It has been a week since I last dictated, a very rough week. I am not sure how much this chronicle conveys a sense of dying, but that process becomes increasingly vivid for me with the passage of each day. Five days ago, I fell down and bruised my hip. I was preparing my clothing for the following day and somehow slipped and fell on the bedroom floor. I tried to fall onto the bed but bounced off it and back onto a bedside table.

Although the disease itself is not painful, this was a most painful and frightening fall. I lay on the floor, stunned for a few seconds. Then I began to feel sharp pains in my right shoulder and right hip. I attempted to cry out and it seemed to take a few seconds for me to make the sounds, "Help, help!" Mary and Jimmy came running.

It is difficult to recall what thoughts were passing through my mind at that time. I do remember being horribly frightened, again with that totally helpless sensation of lying on the floor, afraid to move, and also afraid to be left there alone. I began to tremble, and then my whole body began to shake violently. I told Mary that I thought I was in shock. She covered me with a blanket and in a few minutes managed to get me into bed.

After the initial shock and pain began to diminish, I remember feeling that I simply had to get up. I had this pervasive fear that if I let this injury take over, it would result in a more permanent and rapid limitation of my activities. I am not ordinarily one who is able to tolerate great pain. However, in the face of this recent fear, I made a great effort to sit on the side of the bed within a half hour of my fall. The very act of forcing myself up, and eventually back onto my feet, in itself had strong psychological reassurance that I was not yet "down and out."

There is this enormous reservoir of determination to fight back that, until the past week, I did not really believe I had. I do not know where it comes from, perhaps from some common human instinct to survive even in the face of incredible circumstances.

Earlier, I have tried to stress the social and psychological aspects of dying. At times, it becomes impossible to distinguish between my own psychological and *biological* responses. Was my trembling on the floor due solely to biological shock, or did it include a strong mixture of fear? Perhaps this kind of question seems merely rhetorical, but I believe it is important to try to know what various forces are operating on and within me at any one point.

For example, a few days after this fall I became virtually sexually impotent. Attempting to have sexual intercourse with my wife on two recent occasions, I could not achieve an erection. Is this some effect of the illness finally taking over this part of my body, or is it an impotence generated by my own fear and rage at what is happening to me generally? If I ask my neurologist, will he know? And if he knows, will he be able to offer me any help?

This latest fall has shaken me physically and psychologically more than anything that has happened to me since I left the hospital last spring. I made a grandiose effort to appear at the University the day following my injuries. It happened to be my busiest day for student conferences and classes. I was slowed down considerably by the pain of the fall, and I am sure that my poor physical mobility must have suggested to faculty and students that I was not very well that day. However, no one questioned or commented specifically to me about my appearance.

There is something increasingly unreal about my getting dressed in a suit and tie and presenting myself in public situations as though I were all right except for the need for a cane to walk about. Yet, as I say this, I know that it is critically important for me to keep on functioning, especially in my professorial duties. I did have conferences with several students that following day, and I was able to keep my mind focused on the students' needs and my criticisms and comments regarding their work.

In one of my classes, we had an excellent discussion, and I presented some material without the pain interfering with my duties. There is something very reassuring for me in simply being able to continue to function this way. This is really an understatement of the psychological necessity for me to continue to function within the limitations of my illness. I could have stayed at home in bed that following day and perhaps allowed myself to become bedridden. It is probably the fear of this that keeps me driving myself back to maintaining my everyday functioning.

This recent injury, as I have ruminated on it and lived with it, has heightened my anxiety about the course of my illness. It confronts me more with the ultimate nature of my illness, being totally bedridden and virtually unable to communicate at all. I wonder at what point I can stop myself along this inevitable route. That is, I want to have the option to decide, along the way, when I have reached the point where it is no longer worthwhile to stay alive.

I somehow know with great certainty that my neurologist will not co-operate with me in terminating my life, even by failing to make efforts to keep me alive. As long as I am able to move about, I have some choice in this matter. But when I become totally immobilized, it is virtually impossible for me to do anything about the continuance of my life.

I know that this issue is fraught with all kinds of complicated moral, medical, and other kinds of issues, and it becomes an increasingly complex problem, as there is technology to literally keep the body alive.

There was a poignant story, on the front page of the Sunday New York *Times*, describing the "suicide" of a twenty-nine-year-old man, half Indian, in Seattle, Washington. Suffering from kidney failure, he was kept alive by periodic use of dialysis medical machinery, even though the medical institutions and practitioners involved in his care had serious doubt as to how long they could continue to keep him alive in this manner.

The point of the article for me was that all the medical institutions and practitioners could not and did not confront themselves and the patient with the basic dilemma of how long to keep him alive. The young man, who must have sensed the confusion and contradiction of those who surrounded him in his illness, managed to make the decision himself. He simply stayed away from the medical institution so long that he died.

There were many unique social and psychological circumstances surrounding the situation of this young man, but I felt his account was very close to my own situation in that at some point someone may have to make the decision about how long I will live. He made his decision in his own way, and this seems to be what caused many of the professionals around him to ponder their own ethics and values. It was apparently this dilemma which caused the situation to "make news" on the first page of the New York *Times*.

What makes this young man's death universal is that he was faced with the essential conflict that many dying people face. Society, whatever that global term refers to, professionals, institutions, have no answers. Yet, at the same time, they make it difficult, if not impossible, for the dying individual to participate in making the decision for himself, except as a desperate act of escape.

If I am to die with some dignity, this does not seem to be the way to do it. Yet what alternatives will I have?

As I dictate these questions, my concern is so urgent that I feel the need to call a physician friend. I need to raise these questions with someone who can at least give me some advice and, I hope, some perspective, on this question that burns within me. I hesitate to share the question with a friend, feeling that it is unfair to ask this kind of advice from another lay person. Yet I know that my neurologist cannot and will not deal with this question which is so vital to me. And I do not want to burden my wife with it. I only hope that she will not have to take personal responsibility for answering the question as I am dying.

I am now awaiting a telephone call from my physician friend. I find myself very anxious at finally confronting this question with someone else. Death seems easy, but dying sometimes seems impossible. We all complicate our lives unnecessarily at times, and perhaps complicating the process of dying is only another projection of our unresolved conflicts and dilemmas. In retrospect, many things in my life that had seemed so complicated were in fact relatively simple or easy to resolve. All my present fumblings and anxieties will also pass, one way or another.

The more I go on with this account, the more it seems difficult and burdensome. Why do I search out and expose myself into this stupid microphone? Is there some kind of common human truth that I think I will discover in this process? That seems a very egotistical expectation. Why am I doing this? I guess I have something worthwhile to communicate to other human beings. Perhaps the telling of this tale does communicate that we are all more human than otherwise, and that we can and do survive as humans even in dying under difficult circumstances.

It is the survival of my own humanity, then, not just me, that has some validity and importance.

I think of my boy, Jimmy, seeing me literally wither away physically. I see him having to adjust his life at home more and more to my own limitations and handicaps. For the first time, yesterday, he had to help me in and out of the bathtub so that I would not fall. "The son becomes father," at age thirteen. To me that seems very cruel. I didn't want to let him see this happen to me. Yet I am letting it happen, and his quiet love warms me and keeps me going. Maybe other thirteen-year-old boys can learn from him as well as from me that dying can include some reaffirmation of life and love in its most elemental and profound sense.

It does not seem that I am discovering any new truths, but I am learning a new, humble meaning of my own humanity. And perhaps that is a most precious thing to get out of all of this. It seems as though I communicate little of this to the people in what social contacts I have. I am reluctant, indeed resistant to using overtly the experience of my dying with others, outside my family. It is not the sort of thing one usually discusses at a luncheon, tea party, or bar. This means, I think, that though we may be liberating ourselves in the area of sexual activity and elsewhere, we are no-where near liberating ourselves in dying activity.

I have harbored the notion that I would indulge, in the last weeks and months of my life, in some new, liberating activities, but I can see that it is pretty much the same old me who is living out the remainder of my life now. Dying is only one small piece of life, and it is life itself that is worth the living and worth the game.

I had hoped to order some priorities in my life, so that in the next few months I would spend a good part of my daily activities in developing a new and exciting educational program. I do not expect to see it through to completion, but I still hold out the hope of taking part in the beginning of a new educational program. This may be related to my need, as my own *ending* approaches, to simultaneously take part in the *beginning* of something else. Is this just another aspect of fulfilling a wish to be perpetuated beyond one's own time?

My firm answer to that now is, What difference does it make what the motivation may be? The idea in itself gives me much to do and stimulates me beyond simply engaging in day-to-day activity. And the promise of taking part in something much more exciting is a part of the hopefulness I need.

It seems to me that another thing I am learning as this narrative goes on is that this recounting of my daily life and tribulations is much less important to me than is living that life, and less important than direct interaction and communication with other human beings. Although a good part of my life has been spent in this kind of introspective and academic endeavor and I have learned to discipline myself in isolated scholarly work, life is better lived than written about.

Perhaps this is why many dying people do not carry out attempts to maintain diaries or otherwise to recount in any great detail the process of their dying. Yet I am committed to setting down this account and I will pursue it relentlessly, although perhaps with ambivalence. I don't have the foggiest notion whether anyone will hear these words, let alone read them at some time in the future. However, I wouldn't be setting them down unless I had *some* hope that they would be read.

This week, I will be going to the seminar on dying to describe the experience of dying as I have known it. This has been worrying away in the back of my mind, mainly because I have been very fearful of discussing the full implications of my illness with others. More specifically, I have been unable to face and to discuss the final stage of the illness. I expect in the seminar that I will be asked to discuss this. (If I preferred, I could simply decline to talk about it.

However, I take it as something of a challenge to face my own feelings and to be able to discuss the subject with others. This may be the benefit I can extract for myself out of the seminar.)

Focusing more narrowly, I see the problem as my difficulty in facing the thought of being in a hospital bed, for an indeterminate length of time, able to see and hear and think but almost literally unable to do anything else. With modern technology, it is conceivable that I could be kept alive under these conditions for a very long time. First, the general idea remains appalling to me. Second, the fantastic expense that may mount up in keeping me alive in this form is absolutely intolerable to me. My dilemma is that I simply do not know that I can do anything to prevent this situation. And if I knew I could do something about it, I do not know what I would do. Maybe this is what I have to face the seminar, and thus to face myself, with.

I am anxious about that seminar; it is as though I have to take it on, to somehow prove to myself that I can face my fears. This may be characteristic of my general life style and one of the reasons why I persist in this narrative. There is a force within me that keeps me fighting to live, and my childlike curiosity wants to examine and scrutinize and come face to face with that peculiar force within me.

Recalling Franklin Roosevelt, I have nothing to fear but fear itself. Increasingly, there seems nothing fearful about dying, nor about death itself. There are fearful circumstances and events along the way, but this is not substantially different from a variety of fears I have had throughout my life.

What seems different is this indomitable will to live in the face of depressing and discouraging circumstances. The vigor for survival must have always been there, but now it is something that is brought more clearly to the test and becomes a more visible part of myself. I find it most amazing at this point in my life, and I hope to be able to describe, analyze, and understand more of it as time goes on. If I do, you will be hearing more about it from me.

I will retreat from this isolated recording for another week, and return to this machine to try to recount further my unique experiences with living and dying.

# CHAPTER FOURTEEN

# *Impact on Others*

---

It was a very full week and I have another busy one coming up. I received a letter from some publishers of academic material on dying; they were not interested in publishing this manuscript. That has strengthened my determination to see that it does become published in book form at some time. Particularly the events of the past week have convinced me that there is a need for having this account available to some readership.

I attended the seminar on dying last week. The seminar included theological students, medical students, and graduate social-work students, about fifteen to twenty people. I recounted my seven days in the hospital, much as I have recorded here earlier. A tape recording was made, which I hope to incorporate into this book.

I had hoped for some interaction, including a question-and-answer period, but the recounting of my days in the hospital seemed to take up nearly all of the time. During this monologue the seminar members were very intense and quiet, appearing to be listening to my every word. I had not expected my narrative to have such impact.

As I recounted the events, a few recollections were conveyed with strong feeling. I had expected that. It was late on a very busy day for me, and I felt very tired when the seminar concluded. The professor suggested that I return in two weeks to discuss questions the members might have. We spent a few minutes identifying some questions or areas they would like me to elaborate upon. The professor intends to have the seminar discuss in the intervening period their reactions to my first presentation. This makes sense in the light of the intense, non-verbal response demonstrated during my monologue.*

It is interesting to note some of the responses on the part of the faculty involved in the seminar. At the end, a professor of psychiatry commented about the impact of technology in separating the physician from the patient. While this was a very sound observation, it definitely served to create some distance between him and the intensity of the meeting. A professor of theology followed me out of the building, seeming to be very quiet and thoughtful, even somewhat shaken. Perhaps I did not leave these men with any firm grasp on what they could do, although it was not my intent to undercut or attack their professional roles and responsibilities.

The major professor in the seminar came to me the following day to let me know of the great emotional impact of the meeting. He wanted to discuss the need of some of our colleagues to deny death and dying. He cited two specific people who had not attended the seminar. I could agree with his statement of the one colleague's need to deny my terminal illness. I happened to know that the other person had had surgery for suspected malignant growths. The seminar leader knew nothing about this but reported that the

---

* Editor's note: The December 1971 seminar discussed in this chapter was the one that generated "Notes of a Dying Professor" (op. cit.). Instead of including either the tape transcript or the published article, we have used parts as footnotes. Two weeks after his first appearance at the seminar, Archie returned for the questions and answers. They are reprinted in our Appendix, "Excerpts from Seminar I." The material retains a fresh slant even where Archie was dealing with issues previously mentioned in this diary.

man had engaged in some banter with him about jokes and cartoons on dying. The seminar professor was, I thought, overeager to make psychological interpretations about our colleague.

There is another aspect here that I did not raise with the seminar leader. The two colleagues he was talking about are both Jewish. There is something of special cultural significance in attitudes and behavior toward dying. I cannot claim to be an expert on the Jewish culture and dying, but I do know that Jewish humor serves many social functions. For instance, our colleague has a very conscious way of using Jewish humor to describe that which is painful and sad. It illustrates my contention that humor is more than simply psychopathological. Humor serves the function among Jews and many other groups of talking about and attempting to deal with subjects that are difficult or impossible to discuss in some other context. I believe that any good humorist or comedian knows this as a basic tool of his trade. The need for humor is normal and universal, and that is why humor is not the exclusive domain of the psychological professionals despite the implied claims of some of them.

This was brought home to me again recently at a social gathering at someone else's home. I had called my physician friends, a husband and wife, about advice for the stages of my illness when I am completely immobilized. Although I am not to meet them professionally for a few days, we were all at the home of some friends during the past weekend. The husband-physician dominated the conversation during the first part of the evening by joking about sex and illness. I read into that banter some tension and discomfort on his part in having to deal with me in a few days regarding my illness.

It does seem I am loading a terribly heavy burden onto another human being in asking for advice about my strong intention not to be kept alive when the absence of medical measures would permit me to die. This seems to pose an impossible dilemma for physicians, even when they know that this is my unequivocal wish. I am now very uncertain that my physician friends will really be able to help me on this problem. I thought they might intervene with the neurologist in charge of my care, but now I have serious doubts about this.

I am getting weaker and weaker. I think that I am rapidly moving from the stage of being able to get around by myself to a state wherein I will have to remain in a wheelchair to get around. Walking is slower and slower, and I constantly need the cane to be sure that I do not fall or stumble. Living in a wheelchair will present many new adjustments in itself. It will, especially, require extra time and care on the part of my wife and son when I am at home. It will also become increasingly expensive to maintain myself in this manner.

As long as I can continue to function as a teacher, I want to get about, even in a wheelchair. I have very little ambivalence about that. It will create other situations about which I do have some ambivalence, however. For example, I will have to depend on others to help me get from one building to another. This will mean some degree of physical dependence on my colleagues or students, which I have been able to avoid thus far.

Because of the increased visibility of my illness, colleagues in my department have shown more-obvious responses to my physical limitations. For example, a professor with whom I was having a conference was interrupted by another, who put her head in the doorway and asked me how I was getting along. This caused the first professor to turn to me and ask what was wrong, was my situation getting worse. What is interesting here is that the "innocent" question of a colleague communicates as much to another colleague as it does to myself.†

In any event, there is an increase in the number of faculty who avoid my gaze and in general defend themselves against my wobbly gait in "normal" social encounters in the building we share. When I am able to move about only in a wheelchair, I can expect that this limiting of interaction will increase, as people will try to create social and psychological distance from me. Thus, moving into a wheelchair will present several additional problems with which I will have to deal primarily by myself.

A friend who lives in another part of the country telephoned me last week while he was visiting in New York. He had thought that he might be able to stop by and visit us before returning home, but this became impossible for him. I found myself, on the telephone, feeling very sad that he would not be able to visit. I told him that I was getting a bit anxious about the progression of my symptoms and about how long I would be able to get around by myself. My anxiety really was in wanting to visit with him and not knowing whether I would ever be able to.

Perhaps I will increasingly feel this (so far unusual) sense of urgency to do things and see people "before my

† Editor's note: The reader may wonder what to make of Archie's quotes around "innocent," and indeed, what his real point is here. I surmise, for one thing, that he had a degree of suspicion that he was not ready to make explicit: he wondered if his colleagues might have ulterior motives for concern about his dying. This part of the diary reminded me of Tolstoy's *The Death of Ivan Ilych. The Short Novels of Tolstoy,* translated by Aylmar Maude (New York: The Dial Press, 1946). In this story the associates of the dying man are mainly concerned about opportunities for themselves that will develop when Ivan Ilych finally dies, vacating his prestigious position in a government hierarchy. Archie may have sensed or imagined something of the sort, whether or not there was direct evidence for it.

time is up." I look forward to seeing my two older children, Marc and Lori, at Christmastime, when they visit during their college vacations. I wonder what physical condition I will be in when they arrive home. I expect them to be somewhat shocked by the amount of physical deterioration since the time they last saw me.

During the past week or so, I have been able to talk more directly with my wife about the many necessary arrangements involved in being prepared for my death. Most of the necessary legal arrangements have been made, although I somewhat desperately hope that our financial situation can be improved. I know Mary shares that general anxiety. Details like arranging for cremation or other disposal of my body have yet to be made. It is very important to me to make as many of these arrangements as I can myself, and leave her with as few unnecessary burdens as possible. She is a most unusual woman, and I know that she will do whatever is necessary and see that the children have their own needs met and that they meet their own responsibilities.

Robert Frost wrote a poem about trees, in which he looked out a window at a tree in a storm. He referred to the tree troubled by outer weather and said he was troubled by inner weather. The image occurs to me as symbolic of my constant struggle. I move back and forth between what concerns me internally and what I must deal with externally. I must have some human and social contact beyond my family, and yet that outer world and weather seem to become increasingly constricted. As the outer world closes somewhat upon me, I turn to look back on myself and ask what I contribute to that constriction.

I do not want a world solely of introspection and self-analysis, although this has been a part of me for a long, long while now. One does have to reach out to other human beings to stay in contact, and this becomes harder to do. I am still trying. In the coming week, I will meet a professor whose work I have admired for a long time. She has distinguished herself in the study of medical students' training. I want to pursue with her the possibility of some new interdisciplinary training at the University. Not so incidentally, she may be able to suggest potential publication firms for this manuscript. But my main purpose in arranging the meeting is to determine if it is possible to pursue some innovative and exciting study at the University.

This is one way in which I continue to reach out, but it is also something I would have done regardless of my terminal illness. I hope something comes of it. As I say this, there recurs that inner sense of urgency and uncertainty about the amount of time I have to pursue these interests.

While recording this narrative, I seem to have an increasing sense that I should be getting on with "doing," in contrast to this introspection. I find myself less tolerant of spending time on the recording, and perhaps this means that my psychological need to put the experience down and examine it is decreasing as time goes on. I find myself summarizing in a highly condensed fashion the various events of the previous week, without reliving all of the details and nuances of each event. This may be a sign of my increased need to defend myself, to retain and to build up my social and psychological defenses. It is not a very easy business, and I grow weary at times.

There are a few observations that I do want to record. They constitute a commentary on this day of liberating various groups in our society. One of our more flamboyant professors wears a full beard, usually has love beads around his neck, and otherwise gives social evidence of being part of a "liberated" group of people. I have seen this man several times in the past weeks in our office building. He barely acknowledges my presence and seems to have great difficulty in relating to me. This was not the case in the previous semester, although we were never close friends.

This semester, however, especially in the past two

weeks, when I have been using my cane, it seems quite clear that this colleague is making an effort to avoid any direct contact with me. I make a point of singling him out for description because he represents a general dilemma and a contradiction within the various liberation movements. He is particularly interested in forms of sexual and psychological liberation of the individual, including communal life experience, and yet I have sensed a very personal and desperate need on his part to discover and explore his own liberation.

I do not know how much his reaction to me confirms that his quest for liberation is more a personal one than it is part of some broader concern for others, yet I must note that he has evidenced a strong need to avoid me. His behavior is neither liberated nor liberating. And I find this to be true of others. For example, among the large number of women faculty in our department, some mild versions of Women's Liberation are often espoused. I do not find that these individuals express any particular concern, nor do they convey any particular empathy, for my liberation in my situation.

Liberation movements operate on the assumption of a generalized concern for the human condition, of valuing individuals and rewarding them regardless of sex or race or whatever. If some of my colleagues are illustrative of liberation-movement leaders, then I must remain skeptical of such movements. If they cannot deal with my humanity and my mortality, I must ask myself how much they can deal with their own and the humanity and mortality of others.

I am criticizing my colleagues less than I am criticizing the rhetoric that is often bandied about but too often has very little substance when it comes to specific behaviors. We do indeed have a long way to go before we truly liberate ourselves individually and collectively.

As I said at the seminar, I think my circumstances provide a fortuitous viewpoint from which to analyze certain aspects of the behavior of others. First, I have some knowledge and skill in understanding myself and in understanding other human beings, which is part of my professional grounding. Second, my own life happened to turn quite suddenly, so that I was put into a position of having to live through something that I had taught or at least studied but had not experienced emotionally. I think this combination of factors is unique and likely to amplify the understanding of those who would like to know what is important to the dying person.‡

---

‡ Editor's note: Several times now, we have seen Archie observing his peers, pointing to the inconsistencies between their behavior and what they profess. Each time, I am moved to regret that he apparently did not open the subject for discussion with his colleagues. Back in the days when we worked together, if he posed a problem, we all would chime in and clarify our thoughts. Sometimes we would modify our stand or he his. Our trust in ourselves and in each other seemed to grow through these discussions.

What constraints were there upon him in 1971? I suppose he was too tired to spend energy on these concerns. Further, he did not feel in a position to be frank about his condition. To someone of his essentially open nature, secretiveness was necessarily a matter of conflict. Thus the others felt they were faced with his taboo as well as with whatever conflicts they had, and distance undoubtedly grew. They could not help him to open up what he *could* talk about.

In any case, I believe he would have enjoyed the exchange and, possibly, through it could have enhanced understanding, as he seemed to do in the seminars recorded below.

# CHAPTER FIFTEEN

## *Gaps to Be Bridged*

---

It has been almost two months since I last dictated this narrative. Much has happened. A discouraging development is my increased physical deterioration and handicap. In trying to begin this dictation I dropped the machine. My hands and fingers have very little function or strength left. My fingers are more like claws, very clumsy, requiring an inordinate amount of patience.

I suppose that it was some mixture of the discouragement about my physical decline and the increase in my activities at the University, that resulted in my putting aside this weekly account. The time and energy I now must spend in simply keeping myself going physically detract from leisure time and the luxury of doing this recording. Nevertheless, I will again try to make weekly recordings that will describe my current life.

There has been an incredible delay in getting medical care, especially a referral for physical therapy, in the past two months. Until recently, it was impossible to determine where the delay was occurring and for what reasons. I had asked my neurologist for a referral to physical therapy sometime last August or September. I was referred to a physician in a physical-therapy department, but no actual physical therapy was forthcoming.

I have had the very practical help of an occupational therapist, in the shape of small aids that help my hands function in my daily care. However, I need physical therapy, not to prevent further muscle deterioration, since that is impossible, but to keep the remaining muscles active and useful as long as possible.

While I know that my neurologist has some doubt about the value of physical therapy, he has told me in the past that he would refer me, nevertheless, for this type of therapy. Months have passed without any effective referral being made. In my efforts to check by telephone with a variety of the people involved in such a referral, I got no direct answers but, rather, an evasive kind of run-around from everyone concerned. This led me to feel that there was little I could do in this situation, and I began to seriously question what value there was in having a neurologist in charge of my medical care.

A month ago, I decided to ask my wife to go with me to the neurologist, to help check on my impressions and to see if I were somehow not communicating correctly with this man. We raised a number of specific questions regarding my care and put them so directly that he simply had to give some direct response. His response was, "What do you want me to do?" Apparently he was willing to do whatever I thought necessary but required that *I* specify precisely what is necessary.

Again I stressed that I wanted ongoing therapy to maintain my physical functioning as long as possible. A referral was again made to physical therapy. I again saw the physician in charge of physical therapy. He assigned a physical therapist who would call at my home. I realized later that this therapist was not connected with the hospital but was in private practice. She called at my home once and made some practical suggestions in terms of exercises and exercising equipment. This one visit was the last heard from her. Again an interval of several weeks occurred before I could discover the reason for the absence of any contact. The reason was finally determined when my wife called the physician responsible for prescribing physical therapy. When questioned by Mary, he said that he simply did not see any value in physical therapy for me, given the severe nature of my illness and presumably the short time I have to live. Pressed to provide physical therapy that would help keep me functioning to some degree, the physician again agreed to institute such a program. This, I hope, will begin within the next week.

It has taken an enormous amount of stamina and energy and persistence to get something as simple as physical therapy for myself. I would think that many less persistent individuals in my situation would long ago have given up. If I had given up and not attempted any exercise to this date, I am certain that I would be totally bedridden and well on my way to complications of the illness which would result in death. It is only by exercising, that I really have been able to keep myself physically functioning thus far. These exercises have been suggested by a medical friend who has consulted with a physical therapist. Exercise enabled me to keep my legs functioning so that I can still walk about on my own.

It is only through the initiative of this medical friend, who has done a great deal of reading and consulting about this disease, that I have been able to keep going physically. It is simply a lucky happenstance that I met this physician, without whom the whole army of medical experts out there would have been of little help.

Here, again, I cannot escape observing that the psychological reactions of the physicians upon whom I have been dependent for medical care to some degree determine the progress of my illness. That is, if the medical experts "give up," then there is very little that I can do myself to keep on going. Even though the physicians do not verbalize their own sense of giving up on me, the non-verbal message comes through loudly and clearly. This is particularly true when I get the run-around week after week and month after month in response to a simple request. It is what is *not* said, what is *not* communicated, that screams out, with increasing eloquence, and eventually even begins to convince me, that there really is no hope.

Fortunately, there have been a few people who do hold out some realistic hope for me, and it is these exceptional individuals who have helped me to keep going thus far.

I was raised in an era when the physician was considered all-knowing. During my life, especially in my professional work with physicians, I have come to see that they are as human and frail as any other group of people. However, as I reflect on my experiences of the past few months, I realize that I still carry within myself some of that distorted view of the physician; that is, I still project a great deal of authority, particularly upon the specialists I have had to deal with.

My way of communicating this view has perhaps been somewhat threatening to the doctors in charge of my care. That is, I can speak very directly and bluntly about my illness and the reality of death, but this has not conveyed to my doctors what it is they can do for me and what precisely I expect them to do.

A part I play in the difficulty with physicians came clearer to me in a social contact I recently had with a psychoanalyst. He was discussing with me his experiences with serious medical problems in his family, especially illustrating how defensive and cruel physicians and surgeons can often be. He gave one harrowing account of how a physican refused to take responsibility for treatment. My response was that it was incredible.

He retorted that it was not incredible at all but very common among physicians and surgeons in his broad experience. The point that he seemed to be making was that we impute to physicians a great deal more responsibility and personal strength and insight than ever really seems to be the case. He spoke of the need for the patient and his family to be very aggressive in pursuit of their own survival, especially in direct dealings with physicians.

At one point, in summarizing some of the difficulties that physicians present, he said that the "ego ideal" of the physician is a corpse. That is, the medical student learns by working on a corpse. (Further, no matter what the physician does, the patient ends up a corpse.) This was a clever overstatement to emphasize that physicians have difficulty in dealing with wiggling, reacting, feeling, living patients.*

His comments brought home to me my need to make much greater use of my own clinical understanding and skills, even as I work with my physicians. It is not sufficient to say, as I have earlier, that I will not let the doctor's problems become my problems. To some considerable degree, as the events of the past two months have indicated, I cannot keep the doctor's problems from becoming my problems. My alternative, then, is to try somehow to break through the reactions of the doctors who are critical for my medical care.

One way to do this is to relate to these doctors in a way that is egosyntonic for them. That is, I must bear in mind ways in which I can present to them what I need so that my needs will fit their own needs. Challenging the doctor, or making statements that will make him feel inadequate or less prepared to deal with the situation than myself, will only reinforce his need to keep his distance from me. This is an important lesson. I have yet to demonstrate that I have learned to do this with my doctors.

---

* Editor's note: "Ego Ideal" is a psychoanalytic term, "a . . . criterion of personal excellence toward which an individual strives, . . ." according to the American College Dictionary, (New York: Random House, 1959). Does this analyst, then, also imply that the physician would prefer to rid *himself* of human qualities?

# CHAPTER SIXTEEN

# *Living with Dying*

I have asked myself many times why I am recording this narrative. The question has recurred recently, as I have had some response from discussing my situation in the December seminar on death and dying. My presentation there apparently had a very profound effect upon the people attending. An editor of a magazine, having heard about the seminar, has listened to the tape recording of my presentation. He wants to publish a summary of it as a feature article in his magazine.

At this point I do not want my situation publicly known, because I want to try to continue teaching for another year; I very much need the money. I have been advised by some friends not to risk my employment at the University for another year, and to put off any publication about my illness. In considering a magazine article, there is the obvious incentive that this may lead to some additional income for me or my family. It also could represent advance publicity for the book that may come of this narrative. My only hesitation about having my name identified is in running the risk of my employment. The magazine editor was very deeply affected when he listened to my tape recording and thought the material would have a wide appeal. He was very honest with me and said that he probably had some vested interest in wanting to "use" my material, to have a "scoop" himself. He made it clear that he is anxious to have the opportunity to be the first person to publish this material.

These comments, plus some that I have heard from people who attended the seminar, encouraged me that there may be a broad readership for my own personal observations.

I do wonder at times, when I am referring to people close to me, how they may feel when this is eventually put into print. I had perhaps some forecast of this in the past few weeks. Some friends of ours visited from St. Louis about two weeks ago. The husband is the man I referred to earlier as the businessman who came to see me after I had been released from the hospital. He is the one who gave me some advice and financial help but insisted on trying to clarify with me why I was so upset about finances at that point in my life. In talking with me in the past few weeks, he did not remember that he came to my house and helped me in this important way. I told him that I had recorded some of this and that my presentation at the seminar had been typed up. He and his wife looked at the two or three pages of transcript where I describe his coming to our house. They were both intensely absorbed in reading those few pages and seemed to make a great effort to contain whatever their emotional response was to my description of their help.

They read only the few pages referring to my friend, and turned the transcript back to me, without comment. The only interpretation I could make of their reaction was that it was powerful, almost overwhelming, and they simply could not verbalize it.

I guess I can only begin to imagine the nature of the unspoken conflicts my friends have about my illness. Its potential impact is illustrated in a recent letter from an old college friend, a very beautiful black woman in California, who told me in her letter that it took her two months to sit down and write to me after she knew of my terminal illness. She had not been able to deal with her own feelings about my illness, but she could now admit this to herself and to me. She wrote some very poignant things about herself and about our memories as undergraduate students. It was for me a rare treat to receive the letter and to hear from such a friend.

It seems to be common that we do not say what we really feel and think at the point in a person's life when it is known that he or she is dying. Thus far, my California friend is the first one to put her feelings in writing. I am touched by the letter and find no kind of morbid or unpleasant reaction in responding to her and in discussing my situation honestly. I guess I hope that more of my friends can be this honest with themselves and with me.

However, as I say this, I am not sure that I could have been that honest myself, prior to knowing about my terminal illness.

Without my friends, and especially without my immediate family, I would not have survived thus far. My illness is taking an increasingly visible toll upon my wife and upon my younger son. Mary gets very tired simply from the demanding routine of getting me dressed and being sure that I do not fall. Jimmy has his own life, but he has to help me in and out of the bathtub, whether he likes it or not. He is very gentle and kind about doing it, although sometimes he'll gripe, like any adolescent. As the illness progresses, the demands upon them continue to increase, but they both seem to accept them as part of their fate as well as mine.

I have conflicts about the demands my illness makes on them, but at this point they do make it possible for me to go on in some kind of productive life, and I want to do that. As my psychoanalyst friend put it, you have to constantly keep fighting the enemy. The enemy in this case is my disease, about which so very little is known. But I do know that this extension of my life has been totally dependent upon the love and care given me by my wife and son.

My daughter, Lori, has just recently made a decision to go to the university here, in order to save money for the family and to reduce the wear and tear on Mary and Jimmy. This is a most unselfish decision on the part of Lori, one that

I regret in some ways because I would like to see her developing her own life on her own. However, I accept her decision, because she will be of great help by living at home and sharing the work and worry. Perhaps it is a rationalization to say that this kind of illness is a maturing experience for a family, but the harsh realities do make one face some aspects of life and survival in a way that a more protected existence does not provide. And I rationalize this help from my family by thinking to myself that they may be able to take off on some very nice vacation when all of this is over. I do hope that they are able to indulge themselves and to mend some of the many wounds that are inflicted by the process of my dying.

# CHAPTER SEVENTEEN

## *A Treatment Prospect*

This chapter in my book may indeed represent a new chapter in my life. Today is Monday, and on Friday I will enter a hospital to try out a new drug, securinine. The account of how this drug was identified and obtained is an intriguing story in itself.

I have mentioned, before, a physician friend who has been very kind and understanding. This friend should remain anonymous, because his efforts to find some treatment for my illness have lacked full sanction of medical societies, or at least have met with some antagonism on the part of his medical colleagues. In any event, securinine has been used in Russia and China over the past two decades for the muscle atrophy that occurs in patients with poliomyelitis. It has not been used in the United States for any disease, as far as can be determined through medical journals and medical circles, but its use has been reported in medical journals of the Soviet Union.

My doctor friend obtained translations of the reports on its use in Russia. He also knows someone who recently returned from China, one of the group of American physicians that visited China after the many years' gap in communication between China and the United States. One of the American doctors had learned of the use of securinine with polio patients in China. The report indicated success similar to that reported in Russia.

All of this has the element of intrigue not only because of the other two countries involved but because it was uncertain until very recently that any use of the drug in this country would be sanctioned by our medical or government authorities. Apparently the legal issue has been resolved. That is, with the patient's consent it is now perfectly legal to use the drug experimentally in the United States.

A serious problem has been that securinine has not been manufactured in this country, and obtaining it from the Soviet Union or from China would be exceedingly difficult if not impossible. After checking through many complicated circles, my doctor friend did locate two grams of it somewhere in the United States. He will begin to administer it to me on Friday.

Because of the limited knowledge about the drug, my doctor has advised that I be hospitalized for the first day or two, in order to be certain that there are no toxic side effects.

To avoid any question colleagues in my department at the University might raise, I am going to phone in on Friday and say that I am home sick with the flu. This seeming paranoia about my illness and the University does have a reality base. I find a number of faculty increasingly solicitous about my illness. Behind these comments is, I believe, a veiled question regarding how long I will be able to maintain my teaching responsibilities in the department. To admit to hospitalization at this point would be a very real risk on my part. The acting dean has already announced a series of conferences with each faculty member to plan for the next year, and I am certain that some question will be raised about my ability to function full time for the next academic year. In any event, it is wise and necessary for me to keep this coming hospitalization a secret from my colleagues. All of this adds to the air of mystery regarding my hospitalization.

When my doctor called to say that the securinine was available and that he thought I should go into the hospital, my immediate reaction was to go right ahead with it. The doctor wanted to be sure that I had all the facts available.

He could not rule out the risk of inducing convulsions, which could lead to death, and obviously wanted me to give very careful thought and evaluation to the risks. I commented that I didn't see what more there was to talk about, since I was more than ready to try the drug.

I do not look forward to another encounter with hospital bureaucracy and probably will be very anxious on the day that I have to go there. However, unless there is some extreme, unpredictable reaction to the drug, I do expect to be back home within two or three days.

I don't consider myself a very brave person. But the cumulative effect of my illness makes me view alternative courses of action much more clearly than I might have done earlier in my life. That is, whatever risk there is in the use of securinine, at this point, I am really quite willing to take. The alternative, of simply continuing to go downhill as I am, is not very heartening. Therefore, I welcome the drug and whatever it brings.

I do not find myself terribly hopeful about the use of the drug. I don't expect any miraculous cure, and perhaps this is one way of preparing myself against disappointment. I suppose that I do have some hope that the progression of my symptoms may be retarded so that I can remain active longer than I would without it.

My wife seems equally certain and clear about experimenting with the drug. It is obvious that my illness continues to be an emotional drain on her. I am not so certain about Jimmy's reaction to my taking the drug and being hospitalized. He has made a point of telling me that he wants to come and see me at the hospital during the afternoon of the first day that I will be there. My guess is that he, too, recognizes that the future of my illness is very clear and that any drug that might be of some benefit is worth trying.

The magazine editor who is interested in publishing some of this account has encouraged me to keep this narrative very subjective, to keep on with a kind of gut-level story. So I ask myself at times if I am really "spilling my guts." I raise the point now because my reaction to being hospitalized and to experimenting with this drug does not seem to come across as any profound emotion. Also, I see that I can keep on spilling my guts, as it were, only so long. One has only so much emotional and physical energy to invest in anything. I certainly do not have energy to burn up in agonizing anticipation.

Perhaps another way of putting it is that I have built up my own necessary defenses, including limiting the expenditure of emotional and physical energy. For example, I no longer have a psychological alarm reaction to falling. That is, I have somehow conditioned myself to rely on other people around me when I am in danger of falling. Last Friday, a colleague of mine helped me walk from my office to the University Hospital for physical therapy. A strong wind was blowing and several times I started to fall down. My colleague grabbed me by the arm. If he had not helped me, the wind would literally have blown me off my feet. I am sure that my friend was quite alarmed and frightened at the danger of my falling. I was not, for I have somehow lost this alarm reflex. If I did have a strong reaction every time I was in danger of falling, I would probably be constantly exhausted because of the sheer emotional drain. Perhaps in some like fashion I have steeled myself for situations like the hospitalization, which is coming up.

The necessity for not involving other people in the details of my illness and in the pending hospitalization was illustrated last night, when we had dinner at the home of some friends. The four-year-old daughter of the friends, at the dinner table, noted that my wife was putting food on my plate and that I was not serving myself. She looked at me very intently across the table and then turned to my wife and asked, "Why do you serve him?" My wife smiled back at her, and I replied with some laughter that she had to serve me because I could not serve myself. I told her that my hands were too weak to lift some of the food and that I had to wear a special strap on my left hand so that I could use a fork to eat my own food.

The little girl looked intently at me and at the strap on my arm. All of the other people at the dinner table were very silent; one could call it a very pregnant silence, and it was unbroken while I continued this serious and frank discussion with the four-year-old. My wife then picked up the discussion with the adults at the table, and noting the candor and the refreshing, direct approach of the little girl regarding my illness, she made some comment about how indirect and complicated are adult references to my illness and disability.

Our hostess turned to my wife with anguish in her face, asking, "What do you say?" Her question was a revelation of how difficult or really impossible it is for her to make any direct reference to my illness and to my growing disability. What I think she was admitting was that she could not deal with her own feelings about my illness. And this is a person who has been most helpful and kind to me in the face of my growing disability.

As my psychoanalyst friend suggested, I need to consider the needs of other people in order to achieve what I want and need in regard to my illness. I sometimes do better than other times at this. For example, last Friday I finally had a full-fledged appointment with a doctor in physical medicine, including some physical-therapy treatments in the office next to his. I told the doctor that I needed his help to keep me functioning as long as possible. I explained that I did not expect any "cures" but I did need his help, even if it meant only keeping a leg or a muscle going for a few more weeks.

I tried to put my request for his services, my need for him, in terms that would meet his own needs. This seemed to work very well, and he did prescribe several types of exercises, which a physical therapist then had me do that same afternoon. The error I made with this doctor was to tell him that the exercises I had been taking on a bicycle, at home, seemed to help and that I thought I would now be completely bedridden if I had not been doing these exercises. This was a mistake, because this physician had nothing to do with prescribing those exercises. That is, again in the psychoanalyst's terms, I was not building the ego of the doctor. I was telling him that something had helped that he had had nothing to do with.

This, I am slowly learning, is not the way to get the help I need. This is something of a paradox and a dilemma. It is not sufficient to learn how to be helped in a professional relationship, particularly as a medical patient; it is equally important to know how to help the helper. That is, one not only assumes the proper role of the patient, but, in some cases such as terminal illness, it is necessary for the patient to teach the doctor how to help the patient. There are many exceptions to this generalization, but the important fact is that they remain exceptions, and I must deal with other people, including some of my colleagues, in a new way.

I am learning a great deal about patience and humor as time goes on. Yesterday, in going outside the house and down our front stairway, I saw three old ladies standing on the sidewalk, looking very disapprovingly at three college students who were moving into a house across the street. Their scowling faces, as they banded together to compare notes about these apparently very undesirable college students told a story in themselves. Their attention, however, was totally diverted when they saw me slowly going down the stairway to the sidewalk. They turned abruptly from the interesting college students across the street to this more interesting man slowly making this way down the stairway. They stared at me intently and then would turn away. I would stare back at one of them until she was forced to avert her gaze from me.

It was amusing to see that their way of staring at me allowed them not to see me returning their stare. Suddenly, one of them would realize that I was staring back quite as intently as they were, and then suddenly they would turn away toward their little circle again. However, their curiosity was insatiable, and again they would turn their heads toward me as I slowly made my way down the sidewalk. Time and time again, I would stare one of them down until she would turn her head away.

After several minutes of this, I could not contain my laughter, and Mary and I laughed and laughed at the incredible sight of these three little old ladies staring away at me. Our laughter must have confused and shocked them more, but it did seem to turn them away from us.

In any event, they seemed to provide another illustration of how some people deal with the deviant person. They treated me, through their stares and through their non-verbal but very expressive facial reactions, as an object, a thing to behold, but not a person with whom they had to engage in the usual social proprieties or social niceties. Only my constant staring, and later laughing at them, brought them to reduce or stop their dealing with me as a stigmatized person.

Fortunately, there is human kindness as well as human indifference and hostility. In facing the prospect of being in a hospital again, I tend to emphasize the possibilities of experiencing kindness rather than hostility or indifference. At the very least, I know that my doctor is someone I can talk with directly, someone who will act as my advocate when it is necessary.

One of the fears I have in going to a hospital is that I need to maintain some regular exercise during the day. If I remain in a hospital bed all day long, it will become very, very difficult for me to get up and walk around by myself. I do have this nagging drive to keep on pushing myself, in dread that inactivity for a long period of time will inevitably lead to a more permanent inactivity and incapacity on my part. This is my main fear in being hospitalized.

The prospect that the drug may produce some toxic effect, in itself, doesn't bother me. If it does, I probably won't have to worry about remaining active. If this sounds like a very rational and unemotional approach to my own situation, perhaps it is. It is not without feeling, however. It is simply based on the realities I have to deal with day by day, and this approach becomes a necessary part of my survival.

I hope that one week from today I will be able to add another chapter, and to add one that will have some promise and hope in it. If another chapter has to be added that is not quite so hopeful, then it nevertheless will be dutifully recorded. In the event that another chapter cannot be added, then I simply will be forced to conclude that the journey has been very much worth the trouble.

# CHAPTER EIGHTEEN

## *Since Treatment*

---

It has been two weeks since I last dictated. A week ago, I was in the hospital, and I will have more to tell about that later. Today is Monday morning, and I have been watching television reports of President Nixon's trip to Peking. Strange as it may seem, that trip has very personal importance to me.

A few days ago, a message was left in the diplomatic pouch of the Chinese delegation at the United Nations in New York. That message tells about my illness and of the use of securinine by a doctor in Peking.

I have been getting the drug for ten days now. While it appears to be in very short supply, there are reports that it has been used for poliomyelitis in China. One doctor in particular apparently has used it on a number of patients for a number of years. Much stronger dosage has been used in China than in the Soviet Union.

As the governments open up some communication between the United States and China, my doctor hopes that he will be able to get more information from Peking about the risks of securinine and its effectiveness. Efforts have been made to obtain medical reports wherever the drug has been used, but even the specialized resources of the Library of Congress, in Washington, yield very little information about it and virtually nothing about any form of treatment of my disease.

There is, then, some hope that the physician in Peking may have information that will enable my doctor to use a higher dosage, with some greater benefit to me.

I was hospitalized one week ago last Friday in order to have constant observation as this drug was administered. By the following Sunday the conservative, Soviet Union dosage was administered to me, and I have remained at that dosage since then. I left the hospital the next Tuesday morning. The hospitalization was a rather pleasant contrast with my hospitalization almost one year ago. The difference was due to many things, not the least of which was my doctor, who made every effort to ensure that I was comfortable and as relaxed as possible during the stay there.

Because of the possibility of some kind of toxic or negative reaction to the drug, my doctor had a neurologist on call at all times. This neurologist is a professor at the Medical School, and thus I was visited by a team of medical students throughout my stay.

Perhaps the most interesting part of my hospitalization was the opportunity to observe the relationship between the medical students and the professor of neurology. The professor was a rather aloof man, quite proper in his bearing, friendly but formal in all of his interaction with me. In the first physical examination of me, he had five or six medical students observing. I was examined on my hospital bed and took off my pajamas. The professor was very circumspect in covering my genitals, even though it was quite a feat to disrobe me and at the same time to keep my groin covered with a bedsheet.

When the doctor was struggling to accomplish this, I commented that it did not bother me and that these were very mature gentlemen looking on. The professor totally ignored my comment and struggled to protect my body, or at least this part of my body.

After the neurologist and his medical students left the room, one of the students held back, staying near the bed. He said my doctor had told him that I had a transcript of my meeting with a seminar on death and dying. Very hesitantly and with some shyness, he asked me if I would be willing to let him read that transcript. I told him that I would have my wife bring the transcript to the hospital on the following day.

This young man struck me as very conscientious, a thorough student. In spite of my initial impression of him as being somewhat "square" and reserved, I was to discover that he was a very sensitive and alive human being.

On the day before I was discharged, the student returned my transcript of the seminar discussion. He told me that he was very moved on reading the paper. He said this with the most genuine and profound feeling. I was surprised at the warmth and sincerity of this young man, who could assume the distance and rather sterile professionalism of his mentor when he felt the occasion called for it. He asked me if I found this current hospitalization to be similar to the last time. All of this discussion went on rather surreptitiously, while his professor and the other medical students were outside my hospital room. It was as though he did not want to be discovered by the professor and his peers.

I was examined by the team of students and the professor on the morning that I was discharged. Again, as the others left the room, this medical student held back to tell me that he appreciated having the opportunity to meet me and that he would personally follow up my care by staying in touch with my doctor. I told him that I thought my doctor had quite a bit to teach regarding the patient's viewpoint and perception of being hospitalized, and that it was primarily my doctor's arrangements and activity that made this hospitalization much less of a traumatic experience for me.

The medical student hung on, as though I might have some last words of wisdom for him. His awkwardness and shyness were amazingly human and kind. He did finally say his good-bys to me and rejoined his colleagues outside in the hall.

My medical chart at the hospital apparently clearly indicated the seriousness of my disease and the risk involved in administering the drug. Therefore there seemed to be few "games" played by nursing staff and others regarding my condition, again in contrast to my prior hospitalization. Not one of the nurses made direct reference to the terminal nature of my illness, but somehow I felt much more comfortable in my dealings with them. It was as if we all knew what was really going on and we did not have to deny it, even though we did not openly discuss it.

This hospital was more informal, to the point of being sloppy sometimes, but I found myself generally much more comfortable here than at the previous hospital. I experienced few, if any, negative reactions to the drug and confirmed for myself that there was absolutely nothing to lose and possibly quite a bit to gain in trying it out. I did not feel anxious or worried about the drug itself.

Within two days I felt some improvement in my tongue, in its not being so stiff and difficult to talk with, and my throat muscles seemed to function better, with little or no choking or gagging. These were the first positive symptoms of the use of the securinine. It also seemed that I was able to walk better, without quite so much stiffness in my leg muscles. I noticed no difference in my hands or arms.

Since leaving the hospital, I think the throat and tongue muscles remain improved, although the stiffness in my legs has returned. My hands continue to atrophy and I find it increasingly difficult to do anything with them.

On the last day at the hospital, I resumed physical therapy, since the few reports on the use of the drug indicate that its effectiveness is dependent on a regular course of physical therapy. I was able to do quite a few heavy exercises at the hospital, and I have tried to continue these exercises at home. Working a full day at my office, I do come home quite tired in the evening. This makes it difficult for me to keep up a full schedule of physical therapy, and it seems clear that I am going to have to make the serious choice between regular physical therapy and trying to keep up my schedule at the University. I find it very difficult at the moment to make a choice between these two things, and postpone making that decision.

In spite of my extensive contact during the past year with well-known medical researchers and practitioners, it is difficult for me to understand and accept the risk that my physician has had to take in securing and administering the drug. In talking with another doctor friend, I have verified that my physician did take considerable personal risk in arranging for it and in administering it to me in the hospital. The whole complex of legal and economic arrangements surrounding medical care becomes clearer and more incredible to me as time goes on.

Why should my physician, the only one (of many who have had contact with me in the past year) to even try to think of any form of treatment for this disease—why should he run any risk at all in trying to keep me alive? Yet the fact is that he does. He runs a risk from the medical board of the hospital where he practices. He runs a risk from the pharmaceutical company where the drug was obtained. He runs a risk from the medical society of which he is a member.

The way to avoid risk seems to be to do nothing. Of course, in controversial areas, that is not unusual. But presumably medicine and medical practitioners are committed to efforts to help their patients and should receive positive sanctions and support from their peers for these efforts. What I am learning, which is really not new, is that these professional values and practices are supported only insofar as they do not threaten or jeopardize the larger professional network.

When there is the possibility of my having a negative reaction to the drug, or dying from it, then there is a closing of the ranks to protect all types of vested interests from any kind of lawsuit or any kind of individual or collective responsibility for my possible death. What is totally ignored in this defensive reaction is a positive effort to avoid what will be my inevitable death if nothing is done in regard to my disease. There are many inherent contradictions and dilemmas in the name of medical ethics and professional values.

I would be quite lost in this maze of ethical arguments if it were not for my physician, who has been willing to take the personal risk and try out the drug.

I have no false hopes of a "cure" and I think I take a realistic view of the grave nature of my disease. On the other hand, I find it depressing to encounter doctor after doctor who will do nothing in regard to my disease except to take a quite benign attitude toward me personally. This, I find, only reinforces the hopeless nature of my situation and, at the same time, makes me feel almost childlike in terms of deferring to the unquestioned authority of the great medical experts.

Even though my doctor has encouraged me to do otherwise, I have tried to make a point of keeping his identity secret. I am trying to do that in this narrative, and I tried to do it in making arrangements for my hospitalization two weeks ago. I called my office and said simply that I wouldn't be in for a day or two. However, when I returned to the office, I found that a number of my colleagues knew that I had been hospitalized. This is an interesting piece of detective work on someone's part, since I had told only one or two people about my plans.

It illustrates the difficulty in limiting knowledge of the medical risk to a small number of people. I could probably elaborate some aspects of my medical care, my hospitalization, and my current situation in a much clearer fashion if I were able to identify the doctor who has been very much involved with me.

Summarizing the events of the past two weeks, I feel encouraged but not enthusiastic as a result of the use of the drug. It is very evident that I am not going to reverse some of the disabling effects of the disease. If it can be stabilized where it is, that is, without further disability, then I will consider myself very lucky. I do have to face the reality that I am indeed disabled, however. This is difficult for me to incorporate; I simply do not automatically think of myself as disabled.

However, I am severely limited in what I can do with my hands, and this is becoming increasingly evident in my daily functioning. Assuming that I can physically continue in this condition, I will have to make many adjustments in my daily living. These would include some more realistic balance between my working hours and the amount of time I spend in physical therapy and rest. I have not made the necessary arrangements yet.

It is somewhat paradoxical that I seem able to accept the full implications of dying, but at the same time I am not quite ready to accept the disabling aspects of the disease. Perhaps it requires some time for human beings fully, psychologically, to take in what happens when there is massive damage to their bodies.

While in the hospital, I met a black man about my age who was receiving physical therapy to exercise the stump of his leg. We engaged in a bit of conversation and mostly nonverbal communication as we both attempted to exercise in the physical-therapy room. I was struck by how quickly we could communicate support to one another, the difficulty of exercising what body movements we had left, and a sense of the struggle and need to fight constantly to keep our bodies, or what remains of them, in motion and functioning.

Beyond this struggle, there is the additional battle of somehow presenting ourselves to the "outer world" and keeping ourselves psychologically as well as physically intact, to the extent possible, in our encounters with non-disabled people.

At this point, I am more than willing to try the higher dosage of the drug, but I respect the need to have more medical information before attempting that. In order to get the full effect of the current use of the drug, I should be exercising and resting much more. In order to do that, I should be cutting way back on my work load at the University. I have been unwilling to do that thus far. I suppose if I am forced to do it, then I will.

The psychological benefit of keeping myself busy at my regular work cannot be overestimated. I went directly from the hospital last Tuesday morning to my office. The change in atmosphere and the stimulation I received in talking with students were of great benefit to me. I suppose I will have to choose, at some point, between my own morale and some minimal *physical* maintenance of my condition. I would hope that the two could be maintained together, but this may not be possible.

I had very much wanted to finish out this semester, up to the summer, without any major interruption in my work schedule. I still hope that this may be possible, perhaps through increased dosage of the drug, which may help me sustain a normal amount of time at my work.

# CHAPTER NINETEEN

# Human and Scientific Values

---

It begins to appear that I am developing some perspectives on scientific and human values for myself as I rework my thoughts and experience.

I am not sure that I can honestly say I have learned anything very new in the past six or eight months that I have been recording this narrative. I have met people who have been exceedingly kind to me and who have gone out of their way to help me in a manner that I would not have believed possible. It is also necessary to note that some of the people I have known or met during this period have been totally indifferent to me.

It is perhaps also accurate to say that a few people, out of their own conflicts about facing death and dying, have been a bit cruel or, at the very least, have increased my difficulty in functioning with my disabilities.

But this does not seem different from any other aspect of life. There are some good and kind people, there are many indifferent people, and there are a few bitter and cold human beings in this world.

Nonetheless, I am learning that I need help beyond the goodness and kindness of people; beyond respect for the dignity of the human being and for a just society, they must also have knowledge and the ability to use that knowledge in fighting my illness.

One specific contrast in my recent experience is between the neurological researchers whom I have consulted, on the one hand, and general practitioners with whom I am currently engaged. As I see it, the highly specialized knowledge of the neurologists has been of no practical value to me. Not until my general practitioners became personally interested was any treatment to be had. They are the ones who took the initiative to exhaust all medical literature regarding my disease and in the course of the search stumbled upon the drug I am now taking.

This suggests that it is the combination of a value stance and commitment, plus the quest for existing knowledge to apply to the disease, that makes for productive reciprocity of values and knowledge. The century-long debate about the tension between values and knowledge, currently polarized in a great deal of ideological confrontation among several groups in our society, seems to miss the whole point of engaging in any kind of change or treatment of society's ills whether medical, social, legal, political, or whatever.

Polarization of points of view, certainly in my experience, only tends to reinforce the lack of application of any kind of effective knowledge.

The issue, seen from my perspective, is not a choice *between* science and human values but, rather, how to apply scientific knowledge and the search for greater knowledge precisely in behalf of very specific human values and human beings. The fact that science and technology are often used with dehumanizing results does not diminish the necessity to apply scientific knowledge in behalf of humane values.

From my academic stance, either analyzing social problems or intervening in them, I have often seen a need to integrate values and science. Now the subject is not just academic and theoretical; it has been real and practical for me for reasons of physical survival during the past year.

I have tried in the past many months, through this narrative, to prove to myself that my subjective account of the experience of dying could have relevance and meaning beyond my own, personal experience. That wider meaning springs from my ability to analyze and communicate in both personal and objective terms. That is, applying some psychological and sociological concepts and knowledge to personal experiences can result in generalizations that may be valid for many other people. I think particularly my description of social interaction of others with me, at varying points during the past year, illustrates a range of social and psychological phenomena that apply beyond my own, very individualized situation.

The artist does a similar thing through writing or painting or whatever, and the effort justifies itself as long as it communicates something to others. Artistic work does not have to meet criteria of scientific inquiry, but in a sense our separation of what is art, what is science, and what is philosophy is merely our own intellectual imposition of false boundaries between a range of experiences, and types of knowledge that human beings are capable of generating and incorporating.

The counterculture movement in this country has unwittingly contributed to some of this false polarization and dichotomization of man's total life experiences. This movement, at least in some of its literature, would emphasize artistic and human values to the total exclusion of scientific knowledge and experience. The totality of man's work is as offended by this group as by some of the arrogant physical, as well as social, scientists who claim to have the answers for all of man's problems, quite apart from any consideration of the impact of those answers upon human beings.

No one of us has a corner on the market in truth or wisdom or beauty or the good life. If the past year has taught me nothing else, it has taught me that there is no one best way of living or dying. It has taught me that we are all more human than otherwise, that no man ever is an island, and that the larger society, in which we live, constantly impinges, for good and bad, upon our daily lives and our daily actions, by ourselves and with others. Changing ourselves and our society, improving the quality of our daily lives, requires not only a strong commitment to human values but the ability to draw upon knowledge of ourselves and society and apply it to our daily lives.

I do not believe that I have very much more worth saying in this particular narrative. At this point I am therefore at least temporarily closing the door on it.

I hope to be able to continue to work on some professional articles on specific subjects in which I have some competence and contribution to make.

# CHAPTER TWENTY

## *Sequelae*

It has been over two months since I last dictated. I stopped dictating partly because it seemed that I had covered the more dramatic developments in my illness and my life up to that point. It is now the last week of April. Although I finally have a good supply of the medicine, my illness has continued to progress and I have become more disabled. I feel an urgency to get recent events recorded.

One event that created a variety of new situations for me was the publication of my article "Notes of a Dying Professor," in the university magazine. Since it was published, about three weeks ago, there has been a great deal of response—in fact, the greatest amount of mail that magazine has ever received in response to any item.

I have received copies of all those letters. At some point, I hope to go over most of them individually and present my response and analysis.

In the meanwhile, I want to note the reactions of some of my colleagues to that article. Three of them wrote letters or notes to me expressing their appreciation for my writing it. Two or three other colleagues told me in person that they appreciated being able to read the article. The other twenty or so have remained totally silent about it, dealing with me as though they did not know about the article or about my terminal illness. This, then, seems a continuation of their game of denying my illness and in some cases simply denying my existence among them at the University.*

Among professionals who presumably help people in trouble, there is some contradiction in the avoidance of my illness and my article. It is an interesting contrast that two secretaries in my office came to me immediately after publication, with tears in their eyes, and told me how moving the article was and of their desire to simply let me know that they had read it and appreciated it.

After the magazine had been out for about a week, I had a number of regrets over having permitted publication. The cumulative effect of the various responses of my colleagues, and of the sheer number of letters sent to the editor, was to make me feel as though I had allowed myself to be exploited and exposed in a public manner, which I had not reckoned with. My main concerns when I was being encouraged to publish had been not to threaten my employment and insurance situation with the University

---

* A well-considered discussion of the human tendency to put distance between oneself and the dying person is found in R. Kastenbaum and R. Aisenberg, *The Psychology of Death* (New York: Springer Publishing Company, Inc., 1972). They propose that, among other reasons for this tendency, we are not experienced or trained in appropriate responses and dislike being reminded that we lack the tools for coping. Further, they observe that we fear experiencing vicarious suffering or vicarious disintegration.

Tolstoy, writing of the dying person's loneliness in *The Death of Ivan Ilych* (op. cit., p. 451), also conveyed sensitivity to the psychology involved: "The awful, terrible act of his dying was, he could see, reduced by those about him to the level of a casual, unpleasant, and almost indecorous incident . . . and this was done by that very decorum which he had served all his life long. He saw that no one felt for him, because no one even wished to grasp his position."

and to keep the identity of my physicians confidential. I had not thought about what might be the psychological impact of having the article published. And, of course, what appeared in the university magazine was not originally prepared as an article for publication; it was an edited version of a lecture and dialogue at a seminar on death and dying. I had no notion at that time that the material would become published in article form. My recording here, which mainly predates my appearance at the seminar, has been made with the clear intent of eventual publication. But I have kept in mind, as I have recorded this document, that I will control its eventual publication. This was not the case in the publication of the magazine article.

Now I find I have severe reservations about any further publicity of myself and my illness. I have a sense of having allowed my very private thoughts and responses to become public knowledge and a matter for public interpretation and debate. This feeling of allowing myself to be exhibited is very unpleasant, and I simply want to cut off any further exposure of this kind.

The main positive benefit I have received from the publication of this article is the verification, from the readers' response to the article, that what I am recording here is of interest to a wide range of people and is likely to be published and to provide at least some income to my family.

During the past few weeks, my physical disability has again become more visible to others. My hands are virtually paralyzed and useless in terms of any major functions. My legs have become increasingly stiff, and I have been able to walk for only very short distances. Going the brief distance from my office to the men's rest room has become a major physical activity for me when I am at the University.

Thus, my very appearance and functioning have become increasingly indicative of the serious and fatal illness I have. Again, people in my office do not respond to this increased disability by dealing with me directly. I can only infer their reaction by catching glimpses of stares at me, or occasionally catching snatches of conversation whispered as I walk by. As I have noted earlier, the physical appearance of disability in itself generates some response to the disabled person. For example, when I was able to use a cane, people would react to me as a disabled person much more obviously than before. This kind of change was again demonstrated by an incident in the past week. As Mary and I were ready to leave for work, I fell at home and cut a deep gash in my forehead. The spurt of blood splattered on my wife's dress and all over the shirt and tie that I was wearing. I was taken to the emergency room of a hospital for stitches and then released to rest at home for a short while.

Later that day, I went to the office for conferences and to attend one of my classes. The right side of my forehead was covered with a large bandage, but otherwise I looked pretty much the same as on any other day. What I noticed was the alarm and frightened response of a number of people in my office upon seeing this large bandage on my head. The fact is that the relatively small cut on my head was a terribly minor thing compared with the ravages of the disease upon my body in general.

The people in my office, however, could not control their shock and concern at the bandage on my head. This is a very interesting view of illness and of injury when it is certain that virtually all of my colleagues read the article in the magazine, which describes my illness in some detail. Generally, they have been able to deny thoroughly the content of that article and avoid any direct interaction with me in the office in relation to that article. However, when I show up with a cut on my forehead, I somehow can no longer be ignored, and that small injury somehow cannot be denied by my colleagues.

There obviously are some gross contradictions and complex ways in which human beings deal not only with death and dying but even with simple matters of relatively unimportant injuries to the body.

The reactions of some of my colleagues, who are otherwise extremely sophisticated, have been most curious and unpredictable to me. When I came to the office with the bandage on my forehead last week, I had to speak with a colleague to rearrange a conference within the next day or two. She came to my office to talk about the pending conference, and as we were discussing this, I noticed that she was quite literally fixing her eyes upon my bandage. I continued the conversation for a few moments but obviously had lost eye contact with her, as she continued to stare with some incredulity at the bandage on my forehead.

I finally had to take responsibility for interrupting the conversation to say yes, I do have a bandage on my forehead, because I fell down at home and had a couple of stitches taken at the hospital. I added that I was all right now. It was only after I literally interpreted my situation to my colleague, that she stopped this strange staring in disbelief at the bandaged forehead. This is not an insensitive person, but she does illustrate the extent to which people with whom I have daily contact may respond in exceedingly strange and at times disturbing (to me) fashion.

One of the aspects of my illness that is puzzling to other people is that when I am dressed and sitting in my chair in my office, I look very well and "normal." This point was noted by one of my students during the past week. I had asked her to carry some papers for me from my office to the classroom because my hands are too weak. Since the papers were not really heavy, she commented that my illness certainly was deceptive, because I did appear to be so well and I exuded a great amount of vitality, especially in the classroom. This is probably an accurate description of how many people view me and my illness. That is, I do appear to be quite well, and it would only be when I remove my coat or sports jacket that people would see my starkly

withered arms and chest. The upper torso looks very ema-
ciated and is indicative of the seriousness of my disease. But
few people outside of my family ever see this part of me exposed.

As I have said, the disease continues to run its course
throughout my body. The medication is probably having
some helpful effect, but I do not believe that it is stopping
the disease at all. In the past few weeks it has become increasingly difficult to get myself around the house in the
evening. I have much greater strength in the morning than
in the afternoon, and by evening I am usually very weak.

This means that, during the evenings at home, my wife
and my son literally have to carry me from one spot to another. I am becoming an increasing physical burden upon
them, and it is very difficult for them to carry me upstairs to
the second floor, where my bedroom is. We will be moving
in a few months to a house with all of the rooms on one
floor.

I wonder at times how long I can continue to remain at
home at all, with this extreme amount of disability. Mary
and Jimmy never seem to indicate that the burden is becoming too much for them or that we should begin to think of
some kind of institutional care. At this point I do not like to
dwell upon that prospect either, but it certainly does seem
that at some point I will simply have to acknowledge that I
cannot remain this much of a permanent physical burden
upon my family.

It has taken virtually all of my physical and emotional
energy to get myself to my office each day during the past
few weeks. There have been mornings when I would have
liked saying to Mary and to myself that we should simply
forget it and I should stay home or do anything other than
drag myself to my office. However, when I get to my office
and begin to function in my role as a professor, the day
seems to go quickly and pleasantly.

My mood has remained fairly good throughout the

physical difficulties of the past several weeks. I found myself out of control emotionally only once, about a week ago, in response to some touching and profound comments that my daughter had written: Lori had sent a book to Jimmy for his birthday. On the inside cover of the book, she had copied a poem from Langston Hughes, and then she had made a few comments at the end of the poem. The poem was about the difficulties of getting through life, with an analogy to an old person climbing a steep stairway. The point my daughter wanted to make was that, although the book she had given to her brother was something of a fantasy about the joys in life, there were also painful and difficult periods in life.

When Jimmy read me the inscription, I found the poem and the comments so close to my own situation that I responded very quickly by bursting out with crying. I was somewhat embarrassed to be crying in front of my son at this apparently small provocation, but at the same time I felt that my reaction was very reasonable and that I was simply profoundly touched by my daughter's sensitivity.

As I was crying, my son said to me that it was going to be all right. And again that seemed like the son becoming more mature than the father. In any event, it was reassuring to me and I collected myself very quickly. My point in recounting this event is that it has been one of the few situations in which I have felt a need for an immediate and strong kind of emotional release. Otherwise, I think I have maintained a fairly well-balanced emotional life in the face of the daily reminders that my physical world is becoming more and more limited and that I do not have a very bright future.

There are two more weeks of classes before the semester ends. After that, I hope to be able to spend more time recording this narrative and covering areas and events that I have omitted thus far. I especially hope to express the importance to me of the two doctors who have been providing me with both medical care and a great friendship.

In any event, I will end this dictation for now.

~ POSTSCRIPT

# Living with a Dying Husband*

BY MARY S. HANLAN, A.C.S.W.

In March of 1971, my husband and I were told that he had amyotrophic lateral sclerosis, a disease neither of us had heard of until that moment but which was expected to claim his life in a few short months or years. He wrote of his initial reactions in "Notes of a Dying Professor" (*Pennsylvania Gazette*, March 1972), including his need to talk to someone—a social worker—about what was happening to him. Now, four years later and a year or so after his death, I am beginning to make a little more sense for myself out of the welter of feelings and advice that swirled around me. Perhaps the recounting of my complementary experiences will also be useful to social workers in attempting to delineate which interventions would be most productive for those of us caught up in the crises of dying.

To enlighten anyone as unfamiliar with the disease as we were, let me say that ALS, amyotrophic lateral sclerosis, is a progressive paralytic disease of the spinal cord; the symptoms, of course, depend on the area of the cord affected. Paralysis of fingers or toes, or, less often, difficulty in speaking or swallowing is usually the first sign. Nothing is known about how to stop the advance of the paralysis, and although there is little pain (thank God for something!), liv-

---

* This paper was originally titled "Role of the Social Worker in the Care of the Terminally Ill and Their Families: A Personal View." Mary Hanlan submitted it in response to a request for such a piece to be used in a symposium in New York on this subject.

ing and dying with the disease is a constant adjustment to new levels of disability and anguish.

Much has been written about the feelings of a terminally ill patient: anger that such an outrage could be happening to him, anger at having to be dependent on others, fear of the unknown (ahead in life, not just in death), guilt about life roles less than adequately performed, tenderness and appreciation for little kindnesses and honest warmth—the gamut of emotions intensely felt. Kübler-Ross (*On Death and Dying*, [New York, The Macmillan Company, 1969]) has postulated five stages through which a terminally ill person progresses, stages based successively on denial, anger, bargaining, depression, and acceptance. In our experience, it was not the fact of death itself about which Archie was preoccupied and which determined his emotional state (except at the very beginning) but the everyday problems of handling progressive disabilities and loss of relationships. And in the main the same was true of me. In retrospect, I would say that our life together between the time of the diagnosis and his death seemed to fall into three, rather than five, stages: (1) orienting ourselves to the whole concept that death was imminent and to all the ramifications of that fact; (2) living with constant adjustment to less movement, and (3) giving up on life. Throughout these periods, waves of feelings of all sorts—depression, relief, anger—seemed to accompany distinct, if minor, changes in his ability to take charge of his life.

After the initial shock was past, our lives settled down to learning to live with disability (the second stage). Archie's began with his right thumb and forefinger, spread slowly throughout his right hand and then to his left (he was left-handed). These first adjustments were fairly easy: he couldn't type, but he could dictate; he couldn't button, but he could pull zippers, particularly if plastic loops were inserted in the zipper (he could then place a finger in the loop and pull with an arm movement rather than a two-finger grasp); he couldn't use regular eating utensils but could manage with a large-handled spoon and wrist support strap; he could shave with the wrist strap, and so on. Periodically, I would comb the variety stores, looking at gadgets created for a particular purpose and trying to imagine other ways to use them that would enlarge his areas of self-help, besides all the things occupational therapy had developed. So, in spite of thoughts that intruded about my familiar world disintegrating at the edges, I didn't feel too threatened going about my daily business. I narrowed my focus ("partializing," in social-work jargon), was able to cope, and felt a peculiar mixture of pride in this feat—especially in view of some of my friends' withdrawals when they could no longer face what was happening to us—and of dread of impending disaster.

Archie himself was very supportive of all this; he maintained as much independence as possible, continuing to work; we could talk about what was happening, including my own need to work and be independent; and we still found enjoyment in each other, both physically and psychologically. Life was going to be bad, we knew, but it wasn't yet too bad, and we took what enjoyment we could. Some might call this denial, but I don't think it was, as we also talked about, and cried about, the soon-to-be, senseless interruption of all our plans and hopes for ourselves and some of those for our children.

But that, of course, was only the beginning. One year, many falls, and a couple of fractures later, he became confined to a wheelchair. Ball-bearing arm attachments, ostensibly to extend the range and type of his arm movements, were not as helpful as anticipated, mainly because they were put on too late. The main advantage was to enable him to smoke his cigars—one of the last pleasures left to him.

As his body wasted away, I found my reactions changing also. He was often too tired to talk, particularly by the time I would get home from work (I hired students to care for him during the day). If I put my head on his chest or lay down beside him with my arm around him, it would be too heavy for him—he didn't have the strength even to support my arm. And I found to my private horror that at times his bony skeleton was grossly unattractive to me, even as I had grown "accustomed" to it. Intercourse became impossible, not because of his lack of erections but because of his inability to control the rest of his body; positioning was extremely difficult, but even when possible, premature ejaculation and/or exhaustion at the entire effort made it too frustrating for both of us.

About six months before his death, his sleep became progressively more disturbed. Night began to melt into day, and he worried about being able to get through the one or two conferences or seminars he would have scheduled for the day (we had moved near campus, so students came to our house). I was up several times each night, not just turning him once or twice as before, but sometimes having to get him out of bed and into a chair to bring some rest to his aching body. And it always seemed as if I had just fallen asleep again when he would need to be put back to bed. My daily existence began to change radically. I dragged myself around physically, and I found little relief psychologically as I realized how much I had depended on him for emotional support. As long as we could talk and understand one another every now and then, I could hold up. But when that communication virtually disappeared, at the time I needed it most (and obviously he did too), we both began to "crack."

Fortunately, at this time the physician suggested an alternating-pressure mattress, which I rented and which allowed Archie (and thus me) much more sleep. We had a kind of a hiatus for a couple of months. Without that, things would have come to a head much sooner; I could not have continued to work on so little sleep much longer.

And then Archie slowly slid into what seemed like another distinct stage: that of giving up, the feeling that life was no longer worth it. Looking back, I realize that at this point our feelings diverged, though each of us was obviously reacting to the other. Ronald Koenig* details various tolerances—for physical pain, emotional pain, dependency, mutilation, isolation—beyond which patients may prefer not to go on living. Archie, who had maintained mastery over his life by continuing to teach and writing of his experiences, could no longer tolerate living with so little control over the course of his life. He began to rage at me for seemingly inconsequential things; he ordered the doctor—a personal friend who made countless house calls—out of the house, to the latter's profound hurt and confusion. He wanted me to send him to an institution in Puerto Rico or Latin America somewhere, saying that their institutions were worse and he would die sooner.

Whatever equanimity I had had before began to disappear. The main source of strength to me during this period was a woman friend, a physician, who was not only understanding professionally but a close friend. I could put my arms around her when I felt the world falling apart underneath me. One of the most difficult things about terminal illness, it seems to me, is seldom stated: that when one is most in need of physical love and affection, there is no means to express it. Archie, trapped in his wasted body, could not even reach out a finger to me nor could I put my arms around him comfortably, as he could not bear the weight. This is the time I needed someone most. For those who have no such warm friends or family who can allow them to be themselves, whatever they are—depressed, angry, exhausted—a social worker could be crucial.

Thus far, I had gotten along without professional psychological help—I am a social worker myself and thought I knew some of the things that were happening to me. (All of

---

* Editor's note: See "Dying vs. Well-Being," in *Nursing Digest* Vol. II, No. 5, May 1974.

this, I hasten to add, was within a very supportive context of other professional help on a fairly personal basis—medicine, and physical and occupational therapy.) Nonetheless, I was getting so rocky I decided I had better see someone. I knew a lot of social workers and psychiatrists through my work, but I wanted to see someone who didn't know me professionally. A social-work friend recommended a psychiatrist—he had been president of the local psychoanalytic association—and I called him for an appointment one day (I confess I was somewhat fearful of what his fee would be). At the end of our fifty minutes, he told me he could not imagine how he could be of help to me, that he thought I had done everything I could and that I was facing what had to be faced better than he could have! That was an "ego trip" that helped me for a couple of weeks but then wore off. (As I write this, I feel guilty as I realize I never even sent him a note of thanks; I kept waiting for the bill, which never came.)

I was again back on my own resources. (Perhaps a social worker would have seen my need for continued support and not dismissed me so gallantly.) I knew I had to keep my job, and I had to take care of Archie and at least see that meals were on the table for my teen-age son. I could manage nothing else. Sometimes I despaired at my loneliness, my loss of intimacy (again, both physical and psychological), but I saw nothing I could do about it. I found support as a dependent "member" of my friend's family, who had a high tolerance for an extra guest. But the more I relied on my friends for support, the more I pulled back from Archie. I could see it happening, but I felt too depleted to do anything about it. I remember talking with him about this one day. He accused me of withdrawing from him emotionally, and my only response was that at least I was still there. Hardly anyone else could stand it—people would say they would come by sometime but seldom did.

About six weeks before he died, he refused to eat anything but lemon pie for several days, demanding to be hospitalized on the psychiatric ward, saying they would take better care of him than I was. At the hospital, the psychiatrist astutely realized that his anger was related to his feelings that I was withdrawing from him, that he had manipulated the whole thing to force a confrontation with me: either I take better "care" of him (i.e., not withdraw from him) or he would leave me. Being near me but more "removed" at the same time had become intolerable to him.

Fortunately, at the same time, getting some decent food in his stomach had a psychologically settling effect, and that, plus the reality that I had to take off from work to care for him, helped him realize very quickly that we were both much better off when he was home. He was simply too disabled to be cared for without expensive private nursing. But the psychiatrist's skill in perceiving what was happening—anger as expression of love rather than negation of it—helped tremendously in resolving the crisis. If hospital personnel (in this case, the psychiatrist) had not understood and seen beyond the presenting symptoms, the whole situation could easily have led to Archie's being "placed."

There is at least a good ending after all this pain: I worked for a school system and was on vacation by the end of June. Archie did not die until late July, and we had a relatively peaceful three or four weeks together. He had no more energy than before, but I was home for the hour or two or three when he felt pretty good; we actually communicated better and with more relaxed love and warmth during that time than we had since the advent of our long, sleepless nights. I remember sitting out on the back porch with him on hot summer days, enjoying being outside together, crying as he dictated letters to our older son and his new bride, whom he was afraid he would never see again (he didn't), knowing the time was short but extremely glad the raging angers were at least abated for a while. It was not acceptance of death, but confirmation that we had to be together and sharing what life had for us if anger was not to overcome us again.

When he died, I had few tears. It seemed as if he had been dying slowly for so long that my crying had already been done. I called our three children, none of whom were home when he died, and they arrived within a day, my older son and his wife, my daughter, and my younger son. That night, we decided to write a memorial service for him (we are not religious) in which we would all participate and partially fulfill a fantasy about which Archie had written. We later expanded this to having Archie also "participate" by playing part of the tape he had recorded about his impending death.

The next night, we all went out bowling, and I remember telling the kids not to look too happy, in case someone we knew saw us—he or she might be in a different stage of mourning than we were and be shocked at our behavior (we were at least happy to be together again). But writing and preparing the service took much more out of me in the next few days than I had anticipated. I included an old friend and two of Archie's students in the service, and helpful as they were, I had to deal with their feelings too in all the planning. The hardest task, actually, was to obtain some music Archie would have liked; we were not looking for standard religious music, and most of the people we approached (jazz or folk musicians) declined because of their lack of comfort with the unfamiliarity of the social cues (even musicians don't play social scenes "by ear"!). The service went well—too well, I later thought, when I was described as being like a "good hostess"; when it was over, a group of friends came over to the house, and I proceeded to get quite drunk.

Only then did I have an overriding sense of relief and exhaustion—it was now *finally* over. I wasn't at all sure how I would manage, but I figured nothing could be worse than what we had gone through. Friends were helpful, and as school began again, in the fall, I felt I was "making it" OK. I would occasionally have waves of depressive crying; I learned I would become wildly lonely if I had not planned something for the weekend nights and both the kids were gone (my younger son was still at home, my daughter lived close by in a college dorm). But the weekdays were all right, and I simply relied on my friends on the weekends, even though my defenses against a world of twos got pretty shaky at times, when I would be the only single person in the group.

I found one of the hardest things was to call several people to do something with me and be turned down one after the other. Although their reasons were quite legitimate and reality-based, I could not stand such "rejection," and a couple of times found myself terribly depressed after several calls only brought no's. (It had never occurred to me that Archie's dying would be felt by me as a rejection.) So I stopped initiating, just "taking" for a while. I even learned to go to a movie by myself—it brought on less depression than "rejection" by friends. After about six months even the latter subsided, and the weekends were no longer such a major problem.

There was another phenomenon that diminished and finally ended about six months after his death: irregular menstruation. During the last several months of Archie's life, my periods became more and more irregular. At first there was simply some spotting in the middle of a cycle, but by the time he died, I no longer knew when I was "spotting" and when was my "regular" flow. I had used birth control pills for years, stopping when we were no longer having intercourse (about the same time as the irregularity began). After Archie died, my physician friend prescribed estrogen again in an attempt to regulate the cycle, but it didn't work, and she told me I would probably have to have a D & C. I felt quite convinced that the upsetting of my menstrual cycle was related to my changed physical needs and/or depression but somehow found this hard to communicate. (I think I was too unclear about a lot of things that were happening to me to be very coherent about it.)

At Christmastime, after a week's vacation I felt better than I had for many months—rested, less depressed, fairly energetic. I even correctly predicted the end of my menstrual irregularity (in January there was a little spotting, in February none). And with all the difficulty I had in communicating my feelings about psychological "explanations" to a friend, I couldn't help wondering how many surgical or other physical procedures were performed on others in similar circumstances because physicians saw no other options.

Another incident in this connection seems worth noting: About six months before Archie died, he and I were asked to present the patient's and family's point of view about medical services; this was to be at Grand Rounds at the hospital where he had received much of his treatment (*not* where the diagnosis was made, about which he wrote in his first article). After becoming much too exhausted at an interdisciplinary seminar a few weeks earlier, he realized he could not accept the invitation to Grand Rounds, and I was asked to give the presentation alone. I spoke of the excellent care we had received from some medical personnel (especially from that hospital); and of silent anger felt toward others, who had to withdraw to protect themselves; and toward all the impersonal procedures designed to help this insulating process (this was still a couple of months before my own slipping into a partial withdrawal). The presentation was videotaped and ostensibly well received, but I always wondered. It was almost a year later that I learned from a social worker at the hospital that the videotape had been used several times and had generated considerable discussion, but that most of the physicians felt I was "looking for rejection." She and the chief of medicine argued against this point, but she felt it was difficult to overcome.

When I first heard of this reaction, I was surprised and somewhat angry. My God, how defensive can doctors get! But as I thought about it, it was as if there were a kernel of common truth there, turned around though it may be. A physician, confronted by the inadequacies of his knowledge and skill to help someone standing in front of him with the audacity to die, out of his reach and help, must also feel terribly rejected and impotent, albeit as irrationally as I felt vis-à-vis Archie's death. Looking for rejection? Perhaps. But the finality of death brings out the inadequacies and underlying dependencies of us all, wife and physician alike. And I now felt more empathy with the pull toward withdrawal, even as I recognized its counterproductive effect.

Now, a little over a year after his death, there are still problems, as the reverberations of the past four years continue to be felt. As I came out of my own depression, I became more aware of my children's difficulties, from which I had partially protected myself when I was more depleted. My daughter and younger son received some individual help, but this is not the same as working through family relationships. Their recent confrontations with me about not having been supportive enough of them made me realize just how much I had concentrated on keeping myself going and how little I had given to them through that period. Adolescence is a difficult time at best, and passage is even more problematical when one's father is slowly dying and one's mother is focused "down." At this time, it's still too close for me to have as much perspective as I would like on the effects on them. But we're making progress and are much more comfortable with one another.

So, what have I to glean from all of this that might be useful to those working with the terminally ill and their families? Certainly there were specific times (after the initial shock of the prognosis, during Archie's lemon-pie-eating episode, and in the later repairing of torn relationships within the family) when professional perspective and insight were crucially important. But, over the long haul, the stress is so constant that the main need is quite simply support. And I would define support here as helping cope with day-by-day realities. One of the problems with a disease like ALS is that there is no known medical help, and it becomes more difficult for a physician to see any role for himself. If he gets hung up on philosophical issues and questions about purpose and/or life and death, he resorts to withdrawal—there is no answer, no way to be helpful. On the other hand, if he can see himself helping to make that particular day or week or month more comfortable, it is easier for him to relate to the patient. One hopes that the social worker begins with more flexibility as to what constitutes "help" and has fewer role constraints in this area.

I was several times impressed with the equanimity of occupational and physical therapists as they worked all day with severely handicapped people—some with terminal illnesses. There was no apparent worry about how long a person had to live, how he or she would face death, or any such imponderable; the therapists simply helped a person accomplish something, however minute, that he had been unable to do before. The clarity of their role apparently enabled them to function with minimum conflict even when working with grotesquely impaired people.

If helping personnel—social workers, physicians, or whoever—conceived of their function with the terminally ill as helping with discrete, day-by-day problems, I believe they would have less trouble just "hanging in there," which is really the most essential ingredient. Families do not walk off (or institutionalize, in reverse terms) unless emotionally at their wits' end, and, it is to be hoped, neither do professionals. I guess all this "wisdom" sums up to a simple statement of being available, of letting terminal clients use social workers however they need to, rather than the latter approaching them with preconceived notions of their "stages" and needs. Friends and professionals who are still there when the going not only gets rough but stays rough are remembered and loved long after the pain fades.

~ APPENDIX

Now we introduce our Appendix, a collection of items that augment and support the Diary.

First is excerpted material from the dialogue that followed by two weeks Archie's presentation at one session of the seminar on death and dying. We call this Seminar I. Transcripts of two meetings with the seminar the next academic year are then presented, as Seminars II and III.

"A Life Line of Students," as I have called it, is next included here. Though terribly handicapped in speech and unable to write in May and July 1973, Archie recorded this article, which was never finished. It was published in the *Pennsylvania Gazette* of October 1973 as part of the editor's column, "So It Goes."

Finally, we have included a paper that Archie wrote for the *Delaware Medical Journal* and which appeared after his death, in February 1974.

M.N.

# Excerpts from Seminar I*

DR. HANLAN: My own preference would be to start the questions with the most difficult one. I forget how you phrased it, but it was in regard to my feelings about my family, my children. Do you want to put it more specifically?

DR. SCHMITT: How have you dealt with this—with them?

(Here Archie answered much as quoted in the footnote on pages 20–21 of the diary, above, making his point about "dealing with" as an ongoing process. Then he discussed his earlier feeling of guilt, as on page 38 of the diary, and touched on aspects of his current life with Jimmy, as on page 82.)

DR. HANLAN: So I came to terms with that part of it in April or May. And that was very difficult, because I had some conflicting feelings about what this would mean psychologically for my boy. The other two children were old enough to psychologically take some greater responsibility for themselves. I didn't feel that a thirteen-year-old boy should have this kind of burden, but on the other hand there is nobody who's going to take the burden from him, either, so I may as well take some responsibility as his father. And we do have a very nice relationship. But, again, that was a hurdle for me to get over.

However, in my relationship with my wife, she and I deal very honestly with one another. We did when I was in

* Interdisciplinary Seminar on Death and Dying, University of Pennsylvania, December 1971

the hospital, and we certainly have since. That was less of a direct conflict for me. I mention some critical points in dealing with my own feelings, but it's something that goes on and gets reworked, as any relationships do.

My wife is a most unusual human being. The comment of the social worker at the hospital was directed as much at her as it was at me, about coming to the acceptance of my illness. It's not easy on my son, Jimmy. He varies from week to week or day to day in how he deals with it. There was something that came up recently and I said, "I don't think this is something we should discuss with Jimmy." The point is that there are very few things we think we shouldn't discuss with him.

QUESTION: There's been no radical change in your children's behavior?

DR. HANLAN: No. Something came up about my daughter. I hesitate to talk about my children, because they have their own lives and their own individuality, so I will omit details. But here is an example about Lori, now seventeen and very precocious, and becoming a young woman very quickly. This is her first year in college and she's having her own problems adjusting to college.

We talk on the telephone regularly, and at one point she was becoming very concerned psychologically about herself. My wife and I suggested that she try to get some professional counseling. And just before she did, she said that she had dated her own personal problems to when I came home from the hospital, that her problems seemed to be related to her knowing about my dying, and she had been upset about this.

I told her on the phone that she might be right, but she might be wrong, too. And that she had to be clear that my problems did not become her problems, or that my problems were not used as an excuse for her own problems. I made this very clear. She did get counseling, and she readily decided that while she was upset about my dying, that really had very little to do with what her own problems were at that time. Now she feels much better.

But one can easily become trapped into one's own conflicts. And my daughter was, in the usual fashion, testing me out to see if I would say that her problem was my problem.

QUESTION: The last time you were here, you mentioned that the physician became closed-mouthed and this created a fear in you—and today you said you were not afraid of death. Can you explain those two reactions?

DR. HANLAN: Yes. I think there is a difference between fear of death and fear of the unknown. I guess that's a subject for a lot of interpretation right there. But, at any rate, the unknown in the early instance was "What in the world is wrong with me, and what's so grave about all of this?" Simply not knowing, but sensing non-verbally that something is radically wrong, while nobody will say what's wrong—that generates fear.

I'm sure there are many analogies; the child who doesn't know why Mommy or Daddy left may be much more fearful than the child who knows. My own experience in child welfare indicates that even young children are capable of understanding a lot more than we give them credit for. And when they understand, it doesn't necessarily make them feel better, but it can obviate an unnecessary amount of fear and anxiety.

That's the kind of fear I felt with the doctors initially. Does that make sense?

QUESTION: It does, in terms of the first question. Are you able to talk about why you are not afraid of death, after the diagnosis was made and it is no longer an unknown factor?

DR. HANLAN: A lady once told me that death is part of life, which is a very pragmatic statement. This was after someone we knew committed suicide, maybe twenty years ago. It made sense to me, simple as it is. I have had for some time a kind of existential approach to life, not with a full-blown philosophical and psychological paraphernalia of existentialism, but in a more pragmatic way. Somebody has a sign outside their door here, a little phrase—what is it?

PARTICIPANT: "Today is the first day of the rest of your life"?

HANLAN: Which is an existential kind of statement. I find that very nice. That's the way I live, and we have lived in that sense, existentially, my wife and I, ever since we were married. So that death, while I never contemplated it per se— neither did I ever think of being immortal.

I do come from a multireligious background. I had no formal religious education, but I was exposed to close relatives who were Catholics, Protestants, and Jews. Growing up in California, I thought this was the way a lot of people grew up. I've heard since I've been here that "mixed marriages" are something kind of nasty. Anyway, that's the story of my ancestry. I don't know what, if anything, it has to do with my view of life and death.

QUESTION: I'd like to go back to this business of your early account with the doctor, because I think we are in the process in medicine of taking a look at this. There are many prescriptions around now about how you should inform a patient, how you should do this and how you should do that. I think most of them come off the top of the doctor's head in some musty library. I don't think it came out of the kind of experience that you have described.

But let me try to fill in the other side of the picture. I suspect that at the moment that doctor was being grave and silent with you there was a certain amount of uncertainty on his part as to exactly what was going on. So that you have essentially two people in a situation of uncertainty. I think the position most physicians take, right or wrong, is that they do not want to unduly alarm the patient at this point, and this is the rationalization for keeping quiet.

They look upon their task largely as a technical one: to make the diagnosis. If they don't know what the diagnosis is, they feel there's nothing they can do for the patient at that moment, so they do nothing. Could you reflect on what the doctor might have done at that point that might have made it easier for you?

DR. HANLAN: I think training for uncertainty is a critical part of medical training generally. I think social workers ought to get a great deal more training for that too. But there is also the technical expertise, highly visible, highly operational; you can put your finger on what the technical expertise is that the physician should have: he ought to know physiology, etc. etc.; very specific things.

That implies a skill and knowledge, an art of medicine, which does not have answers for everything, but it also implies that the physician's own sense of adequacy is to some degree dependent upon his ability to demonstrate that competency, that technical expertise. The fact is that in many areas, especially in my own illness, technical expertise and knowledge don't have much to do with what you can do. And when the physician, particularly a highly specialized one such as a neurologist—who makes an enormous commitment in education, training, establishing oneself in practice—then arrives at a point with a patient where you are confronted with the fact that all your technical knowledge, all the awards you received, is worth—what? What do you know? What can you do about it? You can give it a label. The diagnosis does not generate a predictive prognosis. It generates absolutely no treatment. It generates a tremendous amount of uncertainty.

And that puts the highly trained physician in a particularly vulnerable position. How in the world can he justify himself, his own adequacy, when he is confronted with a situation about which all his technical knowledge and skill is useless? I think it is an inherent dilemma. I don't know any way out of it.

PARTICIPANT: Particularly in neurology. Which accounts for 60–70 per cent of what they do: nothing. But be that as it may, what you mentioned repeatedly was the dehumanizing process. I think neurologists handle their anxieties by becoming rather esoteric. They regard themselves as the scholars in medicine. Their feeling of esteem comes from their ability to rack up a certain number of esoteric diagnoses that most people would miss.

As you say, that presents a dilemma for them. But I think it also tends to remove the patient from them, to make the patient much more of a specimen or a disease entity rather than a person.

DR. HANLAN: I really didn't mean to single out the neurologist in terms of his impact upon me being dehumanized, although I had a tremendous hostility that was projected onto one or two neurologists early in the game. I have little ambivalence about that. But that's *my* problem.

There is a broader point, that goes much beyond the dilemma that those particular neurologists were confronted with by my illness: the dehumanizing aspect of the hospital generally. I think my own case illustrates that it's not a matter of any one physician, but it's the total impact of the hospital, of the whole system, and a variety of people. It's the reinforcement from many sectors upon the patient. I stress that because I think we have to move beyond working through the feelings of a neurologist about dealing with a dying patient. While that's important, and I think Kübler-Ross makes a tremendous contribution toward understanding the importance of that, my view is that it's important to move also into dealing with the impact of the system on the patient. People could have intervened despite the individual conflicts or the need of individuals to deny my dying. The social worker did, but I happened to be in a special position to have one. It counteracted some of this, but I think I still conveyed to you earlier the feeling of being dehumanized.

I guess the point I would make is that it's terribly important to be able to deal with the system. I'm very familiar with a lot of psychiatric literature on attempts to reform the psychiatric hospital, to deal with it as a social system. I have a strong conviction that it is important to deal at this level, in terms of patient care, as well as at the level of individual treatment of the patient.

From my point of view, it is not sufficient to have individual professionals able to cope with their own feelings. We cannot leave it at that. One must somehow intervene in the whole system of care.†

---

† Editor's note: Seventeen months later, Archie recorded for classroom use material about patients' rights. "In the Philadelphia hospital the nurses and physical therapists were very humane and helpful, and some were very skilled. It's important to note, nonetheless, that the rights of patients continue to be violated even under the best of conditions. That's not because of 'good guys' and 'bad guys' or victimizers and victims. The system itself is beyond the good or bad intentions of individuals. Individuals get caught in the system and behave according to the expectations sanctioned, behave beyond their own intent. That happens every day in every hospital.

"I have described earlier being socialized to the role of the patient as I went into the hospital in another city two years ago. The admissions procedures were particularly difficult to accept. They were a kind of Alice-in-Wonderland experience. I was told I had to guarantee payment for services not yet rendered: yet no one (especially me) knew the nature of the services to be given. This kind of thing also happens in Philadelphia. A few days ago, I heard the commissioner of insurance say quite unequivocally that it is illegal to require patients to advance money prior to admission. He would be willing to try to obtain legal action in such cases. It seems to me there are a number of points in the health-

(Question concerning relationships with the children)

DR. HANLAN: Well, there was Lori on the phone, and I dealt with that situation. I think it has in some ways freed her to go ahead. Actually, I don't see much of the two older children now, except during holidays. Marc, now nineteen,

---

care system at which an individual may encounter violations of basic civil rights."

(In regard to the American Hospital Association's policies on the patients' bill of rights):

"Unless there is a strong, clear-cut legal basis for saying that these are inalienable rights of any patient, a declaration of policy means very little. Rights are not granted as a charity by doctors or whomever; they are fundamental, and the professional has no choice but to honor them.

"Many patients are quite frightened. I know of a young woman who went to an outpatient clinic here for a follow-up exam. She was told on arrival that she would be examined by a number of doctors and medical students because of her unusual condition. Without further warning, her clothing was removed and she was taken before ten medical men. She felt very frightened and confused. This had not been her understanding of why she was there. From my point of view, she and others have a basic human right to protection from that sort of thing, by legal action if necessary. From her point of view, she doesn't want to make trouble. She is afraid to complain about it, afraid the nurse might be blamed, because she is the 'low person on the totem pole,' afraid her doctor might retaliate against her. It is one minor illustration of how patients' rights are commonly violated.

"The Women's Liberation Movement has made us aware of the treatment of women as objects. I agree with their position, but I think their argument doesn't go far enough. In medical care, men as well as women are treated as objects. We all need to be treated as persons, and that is a fundamental right of the patient."

(FROM AN UNPUBLISHED TRANSCRIPTION.)

had his problems in achieving autonomy and identity, but he's several stages beyond where my daughter is. There's been nothing specific; when he was home, we discussed my illness and dealt with it very directly.

In fact, I don't know whether this elaborates what you're asking for, but he brought a girl friend home in September, and one of the things they did was to put some carpeting on the stairway. I can't do that kind of work any more. And I was falling at that point in time, and one of the concerns my wife had was falling on that stairway. So he and his friend nailed down some carpeting. I guess this was a kind of symbolic gesture.

QUESTION: Was his coming home with a girl friend a symbolic gesture too?

DR. HANLAN: Yes; well, girl friends aren't that new in his life. He has brought girls home before, but not from college.

PARTICIPANT: I get the feeling that you are calling for a more humane or humanistic approach that people should have to other people. I see everything becoming more complex in almost a spiral effect, and the hospital is really an instrument of the society—

DR. HANLAN: At one level, I'd agree. At another level, I wouldn't.

PARTICIPANT: It's there because it serves a need. Do you see any place to stop this cycle?

DR. HANLAN: I think we have to be careful in talking about institutions, hospitals, in viewing them as instruments of society, because, again, we reify them, we impute a reality and importance to some of those analytic constructs that mislead us in some ways. I have a strong analytical bent, but, at the same time, I'm very concerned about the utility of these analytic constructs and how they apply to people.

Talking about hospitals as instruments of society can become quite rhetorical. What is the utility of that for changing what happens to people, or making the hospitals more humanistic, less dehumanizing? It's the people in the hospitals who make it dehumanizing, not society. The people in the hospital are a reflection of the society, of societal values and norms, and their perception of their roles in the hospital may be a reflection of the larger society. But the nitty-gritty is that there are people there, people who treated me like I wasn't a human being. It's those people who have to change. Still, while we focus on the necessary change in people, we must retain a view of the hospital structurally, as an institution, and change that, too.

QUESTION: How do you change that?

DR. HANLAN: Well, there have been a number of experiments in radically changing psychiatric hospitals. I don't want to hold forth on the reform of psychiatric hospitals, which started in England at the end of World War II. There are problems, and we have been able to identify some of the limits of reform in psychiatric hospitals, but we know a great deal about how to go about reforming hospitals as systems.

. . . .

PARTICIPANT: Some doctors are very reluctant to tell a patient that he's going to die or to place a time limit on their life. Did you ever wish that that time limit was not presented to you?

DR. HANLAN: I asked for a specific statement to be given to me when I was being discharged from the hospital. And the best statement the neurologist could give me at that time was six months to three years. I've been told by other neurologists and physicians that there's insufficient evidence to make any such statement. They could say it's terminal, but where he dredged up six months to three years, nobody seems to know, unless he took a mean of all patients from the first diagnosis to death.

At any rate, that six-months-to-three-years thing, while

it came as a blow, doesn't bother me now as much as that the best medical information I can get is that that's a kind of meaningless statement, because there is so little knowledge about the illness, and there is absolutely no predictability except that there is a progression; the rate of it is unknown.

PARTICIPANT: Do they offer any hope that there might be a cure?

DR. HANLAN: No. A lot of lay people say, "Maybe they'll find something."

PARTICIPANT: This is one of Kübler-Ross's recommendations, that the hope always be kept there.

DR. HANLAN: Yes. But the hope factor, for me, is quite different from false reassurance that medical science is going to come thundering down next year— That's really distasteful to me. I can have hope, I can live with hope in terms of enjoying life and hoping to live as long as I can, without having to latch onto the idea that somebody in his little laboratory is going to come up with something. To me that's very unrealistic.

I've been very influenced by Frankl, the Viennese existential psychoanalyst, on the importance of hope. I read it when it first came out, in the late forties. But to me that's very different from having to have a belief or a faith that they will miraculously find a cure for my illness. I can have hope and faith in living. If something comes along, that's great. Maintaining a sense of hope *is* important psychologically.

# Seminar II*

Now Archie's failing strength was devoted to his further work, some of it on this same subject, and to the arduous tasks of daily living, including frequent trips with Mary to physical therapy. In the fall, he resumed full-time teaching (including graduate seminars in administration) and counseling of students. In November, he again met with the University's interdisciplinary seminar on death and dying, this time at home, and the session was tape-recorded. Although that dialogue was based on the diary, it had been reworked in the course of six to seven months. I have included it here almost in its entirety, thinking that its flavor should be enjoyed. Archie was very much alive at this point, more vividly so among students than some of the time when he was dictating alone in his home. We here get a chance to see how his work could indeed feed his morale.

The record of this seminar gave birth to another article, published in the *Pennsylvania Gazette* in February 1973, this time showing his name and entitled "More Notes of a Dying Professor."

M.N.

CHAIRMAN: I don't think that Dr. Archie Hanlan needs an introduction. We all received copies of the *Gazette* article, and I assume we all have read it.

---

* Transcript of Dr. Archie Hanlan's November 1972 meeting with the interdisciplinary seminar on death and dying at the University of Pennsylvania.

DR. HANLAN: I haven't prepared anything special today, but I have given some thought to meeting with you. First, if my voice gives out, I'll try a sip of water, and if that doesn't work, I'll leave you to discuss by yourselves while I rest elsewhere in the house. I don't assume that will happen, but I want you to know it's nothing personal if I do suddenly leave.

Also, there's another possibility that I guess you should be aware of. Sometimes, particularly where there's a lot of smoke around, my eyes will get watery and quite irritated. I will ask one of the students staying with me to get a Kleenex if that happens, and please don't interpret it in psychological terms as though I'm overly depressed or whatever. It is solely a physiological response.

Perhaps I am a bit hypersensitive about some aspects of my illness. The illness has gone on. The reactions of others around me in regard to my illness become more visible as my illness itself is more visible. I find that the reactions of others to me have a very important influence on what my sense of myself as a disabled person is at any given moment.

One thing I was trying to say when I met with you last year was that a critical aspect of being defined as "dying" or having a terminal illness in our society, for me at least, is the institutional definition of that situation, particularly the hospital. A related point is that the others around me, whether they are doctors, nurses, colleagues at Penn, or whatever, define my situation regardless of how I may perceive it myself.

At the most verbal level I guess one can consider societal attitudes about death and dying, as well as social institutions which incorporate these societal attitudes and behavior towards dying. I think analysis at that level is important. However, as I mentioned a year ago, by focusing on the constricted and negative attitudes toward dying people that one meets, a dying person can avoid looking at his own attitude and behavior, and I certainly don't want to fall into that trap.

I feel in this seminar—and you can correct me if I'm wrong—that you do have a constructive focus on the terminally ill patient. (I prefer that term to "dying," because the term "dying" tends to negate the notion that one is still living while in that process. "Terminally ill" at least suggests still doing something about living.) I assume in this seminar that you do look at your own attitudes and behavior, as professionals or would-be professionals, toward the dying person. And I think that's a very appropriate process.

I think it's important to understand that your own personal attitudes towards the people labeled as "dying" can, in the aggregate, determine a good deal of what a hospital does as an institution, because a hospital is, in a sense, nothing more than a group of individuals. In addition to your attitudes and behavior about dying, it's also important to look at larger-level attitudes and behavior in institutions and in society at large.

What I tried to point out a year ago was that one must have both components, that is, larger societal influences and personal influences, to see what really happens to the person labeled as dying in our society.

Erving Goffman, a sociologist at Penn whom I studied with at Berkeley some years ago, has not done any work I know of on death and dying, but he has looked at how deviant people in our society get labeled as such. And dying people are essentially defined as "deviant," because they are different from most of the rest of the people in the society. Goffman is interested in looking at how people get labeled as "deviant" in a society, from a non-psychological point of view. He couldn't care less about what your personal attitudes are, what your own psyche is or is not. He claims to explain critical phenomena on the basis of societal definitions of individuals and situations. I think that's a bit too non-psychological, but it's an important point of view that the very psychologically oriented individual does not often get. Well, that's all very abstract and not very directly related to what has happened to me in the last year. (My voice is getting a bit tired, so I want to pause and get some response from you in a moment.)

I've been hospitalized three times this year: in January, in April, in May. In January, when my disease progressed very rapidly and I began to become noticeably handicapped, when the disease began to affect my walking and limited the use of my arms and hands, my doctors, a husband-and-wife team who are not specialists in the field of neurology, decided to hospitalize me and try a new drug that had been used in the Soviet Union for poliomyelitis. I'm the only person in this country using this drug at the moment. It's no cure, but it has absolutely no side effects, and it does enable me to function within some limits.

At any rate, I was hospitalized at Presbyterian for a week for the initial administration of that drug—I take it by injection every morning. I was hospitalized again in April: I fell at my home and lacerated the side of my head. My gait obviously was becoming impeded by that time. Anyway, I fell at home and had to go into the emergency ward for four or five stitches. About a week later, I fell again, in my office at school, which has a hard, cement, linoleum-covered floor, and broke three or four bones in my face, and my right hand was broken; I was hospitalized then for about a week, just to mend my broken bones.

I returned to school and finished up the semester and was hospitalized in May, this time to begin a period of physical therapy, first in the hospital and then on an out-patient basis, and I've been taking regular physical therapy three times a week ever since.

I better stop at that and catch my breath and get some reaction from you.

QUESTION: [Inaudible]

DR. HANLAN: The most vivid thing is that any time I go out of this house it's, of course, in this wheelchair now, and as you know, Forty-second Street is right outside my door. A lot of traffic. And all I have to do is appear in this wheelchair on that sidewalk and some of the traffic will stop, quite literally. That's one piece of evidence that I'm more noticeble to some people than I was a year ago.

If I stand, with help, as I can, that causes a great deal of public attention. I'm not sure how weird or strange I look standing up, except for the way somebody has to support me—even as I have to describe myself to you, I have to stop and think what do I look like. Part of becoming disabled is that one does not automatically at any one point take on the self-image of being disabled, nor necessarily assume the image other people have. While I don't deny I have severe physical limitations, I don't go around thinking about it all the time. If you saw me do it, you'd certainly see it as a very strange, uncommon way of walking, but I do not automatically think of it that way myself.

QUESTION: Your self-image is continuously out of date.

DR. HANLAN: Yes, to some degree. And one dynamic for me is that I will not accept your or some other person's definition of what that image is or should be. I won't deny certain realities. On the other hand, if, as Goffman says, I allow anyone else to define my own situation, that's not good enough for me. In many situations it will be a very negative, stigmatized, stereotyped point of view. And I don't have to accept that definition.

QUESTION: Are you still teaching?

DR. HANLAN: Yes, with some effort, as you can tell. I had a class here from two to three-fifteen; I'm a bit more tired at this time of day than usual. But I'm teaching full time. I have one class here at home on Wednesday, and I usually go in to Penn on Thursday for a class and student conferences. Then, I have individual conferences here other days of the week. We rented this house this summer precisely because it would allow me to have students at my home when I could not get to my office. Also, it's a single floor. We lived in a two-story house, and I could not manage the stairs by the middle of the summer.

QUESTION: Has your attitude changed since you [inaudible]?

DR. HANLAN: That's a good one. I have to stop and think. A student asked me yesterday—I was having a conference with a doctoral student—and he asked me about my illness. He had read my article. He was expressing how hard it must be for me to continue to teach and so on. I said yes, it is difficult. What I realized, as he fumbled around, was his difficulty in coming to terms with my illness.

Well, sure it's hard, but so are a lot of things. And it isn't all that difficult for me, frankly, at this point. And I must not allow his view of how hard it is for *me* to determine *my* view of how hard it is. I enjoy teaching very much, and it takes all my energy to manage what I'm doing now. My life is very carefully ordered, and so is that of my family. I have hired three students from the University who stay with me Monday through Friday, because I can't be alone.†
My whole life is very carefully structured, and that means conserving all of my energy, planning when I go to sleep at night what I have to do the next day, planning naps or rest during the day; I canceled everything for this morning in order to try to have enough energy this afternoon.

I mention this because few people realize what is involved in keeping one going, as I am functioning at this point. It requires a tremendous amount of effort, not just on my part but on the part of a lot of other people.

---

† Editor's note: For more on the student helpers, see "A Life Line of Students," below.

QUESTION: In your article you talked about your first hospitalization and the kind of impersonalization that you experienced. How did you deal with that kind of treatment during your recent hospitalizations?

DR. HANLAN: Well, it didn't happen at Presbyterian, as it did where I was first hospitalized. Partly because of my doctors here. And I was put on a special ward where the nursing staff was experimenting with new ways of caring for terminally ill patients. Not all the patients are terminally ill, by any means, but the staff has had a series of training sessions in preparation for providing special nursing care to terminally ill patients on one ward.

Another critical difference is that Presbyterian is a very small hospital—and I must confess I have a very big bias against big hospitals. Bigness in any institution, at this point in history, means exceeding complexity and difficulty in control of any aspect of that institution. Presbyterian, because it's small, though it may have grimy walls and not-quite-so-polished floors, can individualize patient care because of the size of the place. Maybe I was treated as a VIP, but I don't think so, in January. I was by April, because they had read the article in the *Gazette* [laughter], but not in January.

. . . .

QUESTION: I think one of the purposes of this discussion is for us to try to come to grips with our own deaths. I would like to ask if you had ever thought of dying or your own death before you became ill.

DR. HANLAN: Oh, I'm sure I did, many times. I can remember as a child being quite fearful of death. I had no formal religious education and was a product of a so-called mixed marriage. I had few preconceived or parentally conceived notions about dying. I never had any grave situations where my life was threatened, that I know of. As close friends or relatives died, then I began to take it more personally. My mother died of a very acute illness in 1959. My father is still living; he's eighty-three years old. A few years after my mother died, a close friend committed suicide, and that was quite a shock to those of us who knew her well.

And I remember then thinking more seriously myself about my own limited life-span, my own humanity, if you will, and talking with some friends about it. I think my article refers to a wise old lady who told me that dying is a part of living; it was around that suicide that we discussed this, and that made a great deal of sense to me at that time. In fact, I had a letter just a week or two ago from that lady, who is now retired in California. She had just heard about my illness. Whatever her conflicts or sorrow about my illness and her aging, it did not in any way impede her writing to me and conveying her own feelings and what she's doing and so on. So she's a pretty unusual person, who can deal with her own feelings about living and dying, knowing that I am dying. And that's very nice for me, I'll tell you, to have people who can do that.

Part of the reaction to my article in the *Gazette* came from people who identified themselves as religious Christians, who were very exercised, very upset, by my article and felt that I needed to be saved immediately, if not sooner. They wrote to the editor—many of the letters were not published. Most of these people—Penn graduates, including Ph.D.'s—felt it necessary to write that my time was running out, and I damn well better do it now, before it's too late. They quoted biblical references and sent literature that I should read. The point is that the most difficult and offensive thing I experienced around the publishing of that article was the response from those people. I did not intend to offend any group, religious or otherwise, and I'm pretty sure the article does not say anything about any religious group or religious belief. But whatever I said certainly did work up some people.

My interpretation of their reaction is that my unwillingness to meet death on their terms, from their religious point of view, is itself very threatening to them; that I have to believe as they do, or their own belief system is really shaken. And maybe that's true not only in religious points of view but in other points of view about dying. Maybe that's what is so difficult for all of us to face: that in looking at our own mortality we may find some assumption we have made about *living* very much shaken up. And we don't like to do that at any time. But looking at dying does mean looking at living and at the way you are spending your life now. If that is not a very happy existence or a very comfortable one, you won't want to look at *either* living or dying.

QUESTION: As I think about death, one of the most frightening things is knowing neither when nor how—the uncertainty of it. I'm wondering how the awareness of the certainty of your own death affects you.

DR. HANLAN: You think mine is more certain than yours?

QUESTIONER: Well—

DR. HANLAN: I don't mean to take you on, but you do assume the end of my life with more finiteness than I know about it at the moment. All I know is that I'm not likely to live nearly as long as you are, but you could go out tonight and get run over. I had a thought in response to what you said—oh, a good example. A few weeks ago, something horrible happened to me: a piece of aspirin lodged in my throat. I had a cold, and I took some aspirin, which dissolved in my trachea so that the granules of aspirin, which I guarantee you taste very bitter, induced a spasm in my trachea, so that I could not breathe. Well, I guess I would have choked to death if the spasm had not finally ended in some way, but I felt like what it must be like to drown, when you can't get air and you somehow struggle very violently to get it, but you can't. This went on for three or four minutes, and my eyes were bulging out— I was conscious and aware of what I was doing, and I had this horrible sensation of not being able to get my breath. I thought, as it went on, God, this is too painful, too cruel, and it simply must stop. I'd rather pass out or die than have this go on. But it seemingly went on and on. It finally stopped. My point in recalling this is that if I had had my choice at that time, that would have been it. But I didn't have my choice about that matter. And when I do have my choice about the matter, I'm still not sure what it will be. But I can conceive of some situations in which life would not be worth living for me.

QUESTION: But do people usually have those choices?

DR. HANLAN: The reality is they don't, but even that reality can be reconstructed so that anyone has choice at any point. Unless human beings have choice in any situation, life really isn't worth living. Life can be pretty bad, whether it's a death camp for Jews in Nazi Germany or living in a black ghetto or starving as a child in Biafra or being on the verge of dying. But life can still be worth living if there is some element of hope. And there is an element of hope only when you perceive for yourself some choice, some alternative, over which you have some control. The fact is that dying patients in most hospitals have most, if not all, choice and decision-making taken away from them. So that the most hopeful thing in changing the care of the terminally ill may be to arrange, outside of our bureaucratic institutions like hospitals and nursing homes, other forms of allowing people to die, in circumstances of their own choosing. I think we ought to invent more alternatives. Hospitals as now constructed eliminate the possibility of providing these choices that are so essential for the patient.

QUESTION: One of the things that interested me in your article was this feeling that people have when they know that they have one or two years left to live. You wanted to go on enjoying living as much as possible. I guess that struck me because something similar happened to me. I don't know

if I could say it the way you can say it, but I wanted to ask
you if that attitude has changed—

DR. HANLAN: Well, I'm doing what I wanted to do right
now. I wouldn't be here today if I didn't want to do this. I
see it as an extension of what I enjoy most—which is teaching, in the very broadest sense of that term. Well, I think
you can surmise better than I where I am at this point in
time. There are not any great unfulfilled desires.

I got a doctorate only five years ago. I was thirty-nine, I
guess well along in life, when I went back to school. And I
gave up a very middle-class existence to go back to school
full time. I have no regrets. I couldn't be teaching without
having done that. It involved considerable sacrifice for my
family as well as myself.

QUESTION: That's exactly what I meant. I'm pretty sure
I couldn't feel the same way at my age—

DR. HANLAN: Well, live a little more—

QUESTION: Do I hear you saying that there is a kind of
closure that you are making and that you can quite easily
do?

DR. HANLAN: Those sound like very technical words.
They have very specific meaning. I think I can accept the
fact that I do have very limited opportunities open to me—
which I have, ever since this disease was diagnosed—and as
my disability progresses, as the disease moves on, there is
less and less I can do. Rather than try to cling to all those
things and not let go, the way to work it is to keep those
things going which I can do and let the other things go by
the board.

It's keeping going the things I can do that are important to me—and priorities change from week to week and
month to month. There is a phrase in physical therapy or a
cliché, "always working with what's left." To try to keep
those bodily functioning going, those muscles or whatever,

that can still be used. And what is no longer usable is no longer usable. I think that's a very logical point of view.*

QUESTION: [inaudible]

DR. HANLAN: I have given strict orders to anybody who has anything to do with me that I don't want a plug put in or any heroic measure of any kind taken, and my family is in complete agreement with that. That's no great solution to my problem as the disease advances, but at least we agree that I will not be kept alive for somebody's sake other than my own. I have very strong feelings about that, at least in my own situation.

Euthanasia, of course, becomes a related issue there, and again, I think patient choice and decision-making by the patient at any point in their life or their dying is important. The women's movement is beginning to raise questions about the woman's right to decide about her own body. Why should I not have the right to decide about my own body in a slightly different way?

There are even more complex issues than that, but dying people are not organized and are not likely to become well organized, so we don't have a group to advocate our cause. We have to rely on others within our environment, I guess, to do that for us.

QUESTION: Do you still have periods of anger, and if so, who with?

DR. HANLAN: My family. And vice versa, of course, since my condition affects their condition also. And my care is just

---

* Editor's note: In "More Notes of a Dying Professor," *supra*, Archie wrote: "I . . . try to use myself as a crude research instrument, a kind of social indicator, in order to collect and analyze participant-observation data which might eventually enable us to generalize beyond individual cases. My motivation is not entirely altrustic, since the effort itself is a means for maintaining . . . sanity at times. We all harbor our inner demons, and I will continue to try to use mine toward intellectual ends."

unbelievably dependent upon my family. I couldn't even demonstrate to you the amount of energy, physical and emotional energy, and time, that is involved in just getting me around this house. So that we all get depressed and angry at times, and I guess we shout at one another. I'm grouchy, as some of my family would put it.

But it's less the dying per se than the realities of living under this condition, which in a way is not so different from living, period.

QUESTION: Have you had any contact with others who have terminal conditions?

DR. HANLAN: Yes, quite by accident. I have a psychoanalyst friend who has a close relative with a terminal illness. I see him occasionally and talk to him on the phone. He told me some time ago that what I had to remember is to constantly fight the enemy, and that means fighting the disease as long as I can.

He has been through this much longer than I have been and much longer than I'm likely to, and in a very painful way, but his advice was to fight the enemy, the disease, as long as possible. He also advised me about medical practitioners, since he teaches medical students: not to have any great reliance upon medical doctors' advocating my cause or responding to anything that might occur; I must be prepared to do this for myself.

His view is that part of the problem of training medical students is that they start out on cadavers (which is true) and that most of their patients wind up as cadavers (which is also true, in the long run). His point is that medical training itself imbues the medical student in the very first stages with dealing with a body and not a person, with literally an inanimate object, the cadaver, and not a feeling, responding, live human being. He sees a need on the part of medical instructors to separate the patient out from the body. That, of course, has a lot of ramifications for the dying patient like myself—and that's what I was first outraged about when I was first hospitalized, as described in my article.

At physical therapy, I meet other terminally ill patients. There is a doctor who has a very painful, cruel kind of terminal illness; heroic measures are being taken to keep her alive, presumably with her consent, although I know at many times she has had questions about these heroic measures. We don't talk about both having terminal illnesses. We both know what our illnesses are, and we kind of console one another when we see each other.

She has been physically much worse off than I because of the side effects of particular drugs. Sometimes she does not recognize me or cannot talk to me.

I don't feel any great empathy or like a soul brother with people merely because they're dying. I wouldn't want to give that impression, and I wouldn't claim to have any more insight into their problems or mine than anyone else. I heard someone on a television panel a few weeks ago—a woman whose husband went through a long, horrible fight with cancer—summarizing the kind of horror she went through in her husband's prolonged illness. She said that dying is the real pornography of our time.

I thought to myself, "Golly, she really put it very well!" We have liberated or claim to have liberated ourselves in regard to sexual behavior, or are trying to do so; we are liberating ourselves in a variety of areas. And it seems to me the one area in which we have yet to start any kind of liberation movement is in regard to dying. In that sense, dying *is* still the real pornography of our time: the dirty business that is to be shunted out of the way, the dying patient who is to be shoved off in a ward where he won't offend or bother other people, the kind of smuttiness about dying where you can get together and make jokes about it although it's certainly not to be shown or discussed aboveboard. In that sense, I very much agree with the woman's comment, that dying is the real pornography of our time. Maybe one of these social movements will finally get around to attempting to liberate us from our own special fears and hang-ups about dying.

QUESTION: Could you cite the ways you have felt this in others around you? You are to many people a kind of symbol of this fear; your very presence evokes it. Could you cite some of that in your experience?

DR. HANLAN: Well, the people in whom my dying evokes fear are the very people who are not going to tell that to me. They're going to turn their back, avert their gaze, start a conversation and end it abruptly, avoid me generally, or deal in a very light, casual, bantering sort of way, as though there is really nothing handicapped or strange about me at all—which is known as "denial" in the trade.

There are a variety of ways. Obviously, I provoke in other people a great deal of conflict and ambivalence. I hesitate to get much more specific than that. One of the weirdest experiences is going out in public and watching. If you see a very disabled or strange-looking person on the street, don't look at him, look at the people who are looking at him and see what they do. You can learn a lot about human behavior by just watching the way other people react to somebody who is identified as deviant or different.

QUESTION: The whole question of privacy must be one that affects you a whole lot. You talked about the students in the house. Surely in the hospital there is no semblance of privacy. Even out in the street now you don't have privacy or anonymity. Is that one of the realities you have to learn to live with?

DR. HANLAN: That's an interesting question. I'm not sure I know how to answer it. What you are saying is generally true, but how much of an identifiable problem it is for me, I'm not quite sure. I do have many long moments of being alone. Somebody always has to be around, but I can turn off the whole world by opening a book. I do that very often.

I can have long periods of time to myself. I make them. I've learned that I have to rest. If I'm not physically tired and I don't want to sleep, I have trained myself to sit down and turn off my mental wheels and relax. For me that's quite an accomplishment. I wouldn't have thought a year or two ago that I could do that. But even that kind of leisure or inactivity I somehow adjust to now, and I don't mean to be any kind of paragon of virtue when I say that. I simply had to do it because I have to do it; it's a necessity. And when we do what we have to do, sometimes that's a pretty good way to live.

QUESTION: Do thoughts come to you about after death?

DR. HANLAN: No. Thoughts in the sense of any organized system about life after death—which I guess is the only way you think about what happens after one is legally, physically dead—no. I don't have any. To me, the Christian concept of heaven and hell and life after death, frankly, is a great bore. I don't mean to offend Christians when I say that, but it just doesn't mean very much to me.

I can find a lot of fault with Judaism, but I certainly do find attractive the lack of all this paraphernalia about what happens after you're dead, in Judaism. And while I don't think the many Jews I have as friends face my death any better than my Christian friends, they at least do not have some of the special hang-ups that my Christian friends have, such as the Christian response to the article in the *Gazette*.

There is a distinctive Christian hang-up, and you would have to tell me more about that than I know, because I've not had any religious education which would explain that reaction to me. And my answer to your question is pretty consistent with my own lack of a formal religion. To me, the question is not an important one, really, that is, personally. I know it is for other people and I respect that. And I hope other people will respect my view of it too.

QUESTION: What is important to you?

DR. HANLAN: Living now.

QUESTION: How do you see your own needs?

DR. HANLAN: A lot of ways. Very personal ways and less personal ways. Personal in terms of my family—and I could give you instances of that, but I don't want to get into that. But I do have very specific things I could cite about my children, and so on. Life going on with individual members of my family is both frustrating and delightful.

What is meaningful to me beyond the family is teaching, interacting with students, hopefully having some meeting of the minds with some of the students—I'll settle for some of the students. That turns me on when it happens. If it happens once a week or once a month, that's pretty good. So maybe I settle for what is meaningful to me in my own existence at a pretty simplistic level, but to me those are very important things.

QUESTION: Except there is a kind of immortality in your creativity, in your own contribution that you are making right here at this time—even your urge to dictate these things into the cassettes. In a sense, there is a kind of immortality in that.

DR. HANLAN: Yes, I think many intellectual people, academic people who have views on life similar to mine, then maybe take a kind of psychological refuge in their work or their academic, professional lives as representing their immortality, because they do not believe in or profess another form of immortality—

QUESTION: Except your being is going to make life forever different, because you have been, because of the impact you've made, and are making here, and the kind of eagerness with which you are willing to do this. It has a kind of continuity to it because it is contagious through us forever.

DR. HANLAN: I appreciate your saying that. At the same time, being the rebel that I am, I have to add that when people have told me that the article was a very moving experience, I have laughed, because, frankly, I'm sick to death of hearing people describe it as a "moving" experience. I didn't come last year to move people. I came in the hope that through my talking about my own experience and being able to generalize a bit beyond my own experience, some other people might eventually be spared some of the things I went through, and maybe some of you budding professionals might behave a little differently in the situation than you might have otherwise.

But I'm frankly not persuaded that simply having a very stirring emotional experience changes the behavior of any of us.

QUESTION: Well, I'd like to add to that, that just knowing you and knowing the courage with which you are going through this has already taken a big block of fear out of it for myself.

DR. HANLAN: I'll accept that.

QUESTION: I don't think from what you've said that death is very important to you, because everything that you've said is that you're concerned with living.

DR. HANLAN: What does "death" mean? How can you define the term? Antonyms have their meaning only in regard to some other concept or term. So death has meaning only insofar as it defines life, and vice versa. So what are you asking?

QUESTION: I'm not asking anything. I'm just saying that I had thought that the problem when you had to face death was death, and I see that you don't think of it that way at all.

DR. HANLAN: Not as a separate entity, no.

QUESTION: You continue to think of how to live—

DR. HANLAN: Yes, and I know that living has a very limited time period around it and at some point I become legally dead. The only difference between you and me is that the probabilities are much greater for me not to be here a year from now than they are for you.

COMMENT: I have repeatedly said that to a group of dying people, talking about death.

DR. HANLAN: We are over the hill biologically at eighteen or nineteen. I think there is a definition of the maximum period of growth of human cells fairly early and it's downhill from then on.

COMMENT: I was thinking that while it's a great probability that you will die before I will, it's not such a great probability that you will be the first one in this room to die.

DR. HANLAN: That's very true. Out of twenty people, you're quite right. So what are *you* going to do between now and then? [Laughter and applause]

# Seminar III*

---

Two or three months elapsed before Archie returned to the seminar on death and dying. By this time, it was co-led by Dr. Abraham Schmitt, as before, and by Mrs. Phyllis Taylor, nurse and community organizer (according to "Learning to Live with Death," by Joan Kron, in *Philadelphia Magazine*, Vol. 64, No. 4 (April 1973), an article that reflects its author's direct observations on this meeting of the seminar).

Listening to the tapes, one is struck by the contrast with the ones done the previous April. Archie's tongue motion was so impaired that his speech was slow and poorly articulated. But he had geared himself up for this stimulating event. He had a message, even a title for it. His state of mind seems comfortable and confident, appropriate to his thinking, which is being further developed and integrated with his total experience.

M.N.

### THE ATTRIBUTES OF A REWARDING PATIENT

DR. SCHMITT: Dr. Hanlan doesn't need an introduction.

DR. HANLAN: I hope you all read the article in the *Gazette*,† because I really do not want to repeat material that is there.

---

* Transcript of Dr. Archie Hanlan's February 1, 1973, meeting with the interdisciplinary seminar on death and dying at the University of Pennsylvania.
† Editor's note: "Notes of a Dying Professor," *supra*.

I get a bit tired by this time of the day, so my speech may sound a bit labored to you. If you cannot understand me, say so, and I'll try to repeat the key words. Probably, the more I talk the clearer my voice will be. It may sound as though it is painful for me to talk, but in fact it is not. So don't worry about my speech being difficult for me, but let me know if you cannot understand me.

OK! I have several students at Penn who stay with me during the week. One of them is alongside me right now. Another student is a graduate in the humanities at Penn, and when I talked with her about my meeting with you today, she gave me some advice. She told me, and I quote her ver-batim, to expect many of you "to be scared shitless!" [Laughter] And I suppose she may be right. However, I really am a rather harmless old man of forty-eight. And my intent is for us to have some exchange here today. I will pre-sent some material, and I expect to get some feedback and reaction from you as well. So, we'll have some eyeball-to-eyeball confrontation here today, and beyond that I hope we'll have some confrontation of our minds as well as our hearts. I expect that, because I think many of you represent a generation of people who have been raised on a variety of psychological theories, whether you've had public or private education thus far. We are a society which somehow bought wholesale the theories of Freud, and you are probably the first generation to reach adulthood where those theories have permeated the entire culture. So, it should not be surprising to find among the modern-day gurus of our society such writers as Theodore Roszak on counterculture or Reich in *Greening of America* with an emphasis on "Con-sciousness Three" or Toffler in *Future Shock*. We have, abounding in our society, especially aimed at your genera-tion, a stress upon consciousness-raising and psychological insight, sometimes at the expense of other important factors; I think, especially in relation to dying in our society, that a sole emphasis upon the psychology of that phenomenon is quite misleading. I'm not arguing against psychology, and I hope to illustrate that as we go on. But my point is, I think we need to know much more than simply the psychology of dying; we need to know more than our own awareness of our own feelings about dying, although that is very important.

My thesis for today is that our society has created a definition of who is a rewarding patient. Further, that definition determines, to some degree, the roles of both the professional and the patient. So that when we become medical patients, we are, like it or not, constrained into certain behaviors. That definition is just as constraining upon the physician, the nurse, the orderly, or whoever is dealing with the patient.

At any rate, my thesis is that there is a social definition of the rewarding patient. The antithesis of that is the unrewarding patient. And the dying patient, in particular, tends to be defined in our society as an unrewarding patient, and I'll try to elaborate on that. If one agrees that the dying person is an unrewarding patient, there are a number of powerful consequences of that definition.

My synthesis, then, if there is one to the subject, would be an effort to identify a way of looking at how we, the society, limit ourselves in the professional-patient relationship, particularly in regard to dying. I hope that there is a way of looking at the social definition which will somehow break up the vicious, self-perpetuating cycle of that definition. (I would recommend, as a very primitive effort at this method of synthesis, the work of Erik Erikson, particularly his book *Childhood and Society*. I have many criticisms of his book, but I do think it represents much more of an integrating and synthesizing kind of work than, for example, the book by Kübler-Ross. And I'll try to elaborate on that later.)

What do I mean by a rewarding patient? Sometimes I'm not sure. What I try to develop around that term is the notion that a patient somehow has to have qualities or do things which make the professional feel useful. If the professional with a patient feels he can't be helpful, that professional tends to feel very inadequate, very uncertain, and that feeling generates a need to separate oneself from the patient. If we cannot help someone, our impulse usually is to get the hell out of there. And that's just as true for the most sophisticated physician as it is for any one of us. I have been examined in the last two years by some of the most prestigious researchers in neurology in the country and in the world. The nature of my disease is such that the best experts *cannot* be helpful by applying their expertise to my disease. That has, I can assure you, a lot of consequences. From my point of view, it does not mean that those people cannot be of help to me. But if, in fact, they define their own worth or value only on the basis of being able to treat or to cure a disease, then I am a living monument to the frustration and limits of their knowledge and ability, or at least, my disease is a living testimony to the inadequacy of their knowledge. So, the nature of a disease, in itself, has some influence on whether a patient is rewarding or not.

There are other aspects of being a rewarding patient, such as being pleasant and nice, following social norms of propriety, and so on. If I were black, in some hospital situations I would be received quite differently and possibly be felt as quite unrewarding, simply because of the color of my skin. I'm not thereby saying all hospitals discriminate, I'm merely using as a likely example a major social phenomenon in our society: white people are generally treated differently from black people. This social fact has differential implications for being a patient, including when one is dying. OK?

I was told some while ago by a psychoanalyst friend, when I was complaining about my relationship with a physician, that I had forgotten the elementary psychology I had learned some twenty years before. My friend told me that I must do everything that was necessary to be egosyntonic with my physician. That is a Freudian way of saying that

I should meet the needs of my doctor. If I didn't do that, I myself then would not get the kind of help from the physician which I needed. I'm not sure how clear that point is to you, but I can return to it later, if you want. That comment from my friend really started some of my thinking about the idea of the rewarding patient and pointed up the fact that there are a variety of factors, some beyond the control of the patient, that are critical in determining how that patient is cared for and what his immediate environment is like.

Let's see if I can give you a personal example. In one of my hospitalizations, a psychiatrist was on duty on the ward all the time, as part of the total staff. At that time, I was very worried and openly upset, very anxious, very cross at people in general, mainly because my personal financial situation had become quite precarious, as a result of my illness. At any rate, I happened to be hospitalized at that time, and as all the patients were, I was given an interview with the psychiatrist. His conclusion, after a brief interview with me, was that my concern about finances was a defense on my part, a refusal to look at my dying. (The fact of my dying, incidentally, is not such a perfect, precise fact. I don't know when I'm going to die, and neither does anyone else.) At any rate, the psychiatrist felt that I had not really *accepted* dying, and I would stress the word "acceptance." You recall that Kübler-Ross uses the term "acceptance" as a kind of ultimate goal which all dying patients should reach, after going through other stages. I take issue with that notion, that acceptance is a clear-cut, unequivocal state on the part of anyone who is dying.

At any rate, back to the psychiatrist I saw. He felt that I had not achieved that Nirvana of acceptance regarding my dying and that, in fact, the reality problem I was very concerned with was not important and was really a smoke-screen on my part. Well, that's all I needed to write that person off, because I knew, for myself, the very real problems I had, and while I would have appreciated some psychological help, it would not be accomplished by my confessing to some dogma, some point of view held by the psychiatrist. What I'm trying to get at is that, in order for me to be a rewarding patient for that person, I had to accept *his* point of view and *his* definition of *my* situation. Otherwise, I was, in his terms, not motivated, not accepting my situation. I'm not arguing here with psychiatry or with psychological theory per se. I *am* arguing against a tendency in our society, generally, to accept theory as fact, to impose a system of reality upon people, particularly patients. And I am arguing against allowing people to impose upon a patient their perceptions, which may be at great variance with the situation as seen by the patient. I felt that to be the case with the psychiatrist.

I might add a happy ending to that experience. I saw another psychotherapist the next day who was more in tune with my immediate situation, and I received a great deal of help at that point around the crisis.

I guess what I'm trying to argue for is a realistic view in opposing the dogma that we go through some neat, ordered sequence that conforms to someone's untested theory. I feel that in regard to Kübler-Ross and in regard to a number of other theories. I think that we must keep in mind the nature of the illness. There are a number of diseases that have a course or consequences which must be understood and appreciated by the people who deal with that patient. And frankly, I am appalled at times by the ignorance of professional people regarding the nature of my disease. It does not, for example, affect my intellectual functioning at any point, although some people may assume that I am a babbling idiot. I may be at times, but that has nothing to do with my illness. The prior life experiences of the patient are critical. And, again, I feel, in some kinds of theory, like Kübler-Ross, that is not given much weight. In the work of someone like Erikson, knowledge of prior life experiences is an absolute necessity for talking about the current state of anyone. I'm trying to think for a moment here, how to wind this up and open it up to you for discussion. I did list a number of personal experiences which might illustrate some points. [Pause]

At one point when I was hospitalized, I was in a room with a retired minister. We both were paralyzed, so that we could not use a call button to call the nurse or anyone else. We had to rely on our voices, such as they were, to call someone to our room. Each time there was a change of shift at the hospital, the burden fell on us to be sure that someone on that subsequent shift knew of our condition. We were the only patients on the ward who could not push a button and call a nurse. I would have thought, after one or two days, someone would be sure that on each shift it would be known that we needed to be checked on. I was there for five or six days, and when I left, it was still necessary for us to tell the staff that we could not call them. That's a rather small, stupid kind of item, but when we were feeling vulnerable and dependent on other people there, it was *very* important to us to know that someone would come when we needed them. As it turned out, my roommate had a stroke after I had been there two days or so, and I discovered him having a stroke. Again, he was unable to call anyone, and well, it merely illustrates the importance of really understanding and acting on the basis of the patient's point of view.

One more illustration. (These anecdotes seem rather morbid to me, but apparently we all tend to share some interest in the morbid at times.) I was sent at one point to an X-ray room after being checked into a hospital, and at that time I was pretty well paralyzed, not much different than I am now. At any rate, the X-ray room was a long way away from my ward. So I was put on a gurney—on a wheel-table—strapped down from head to toe and wheeled off to another part of the hospital. I got the X-rays taken quite quickly and then I was left in a corridor with, it seemed like, hundreds of people milling through that corridor. And I was strapped flat on my back, staring up at the ceiling, which was not a very interesting view. But beyond that, I began to feel myself getting angrier and angrier, that here I was, on that stupid table, left in this totally impersonal corridor, having people stare down at my face as they passed by, no one stopping, being an object of curiosity. And there wasn't a damn thing I could do about it, except get madder and madder. When I returned to my ward, I was so mad and it wasn't (I'm sure the staff on the ward wondered what had set me off) until the following day that I could really express the anger and tell people what an insult I felt that had been. Again, my point is, that it is terribly critical to know what is happening to the patient, even if the patient does not verbalize it, and to know as concretely as you can, what is happening to people before you make judgments and especially before you invoke a psychological prognosis or label for that person. OK? You fire away at me. [Pause] Don't be afraid.

QUESTION: Have you become either more philosophical or religious?

DR. HANLAN: No. I'm not more philosophical, nor more religious. I have rarely, if ever, been what you might call a very religious person. I'm not sure I've ever been what you might call a very philosophical person. I have been intrigued by the Penn students who stay with me, with their interest in oriental philosophy and religion. What I find of interest there is a very radically different notion of acceptance from what we call accepting life, accepting death, accepting reality. Our notion, it seems to me, is very much a Western idea, very much, if you will, a particularly Christian idea, and, I think, very much a distortion of anything Freud ever intended in his theories.

MRS. TAYLOR: How do you deal with your anger? Because I remember in the original article you wrote about being made to feel like an object. And you mentioned that again today, and you mentioned the indignity and the kind of feeling of powerlessness that you have. How do you deal with that, then?

DR. HANLAN: Not very well. As my disease progresses, the range of things which may make me feel angry and powerless seems to increase because my own ability to do things for myself decreases. I have something of a problem in accepting a dependent situation, and I had that problem long before I ever had this disease. This is to say, I'm probably the epitome of the Protestant ethic of being independent, which of course is a myth, but it is a myth which we have imposed upon ourselves in this society, regardless of religion. That Protestant ethic is now the ethic of Jews and Catholics, it is the ethic of the entire society. And I reflect that ethic. It is a dilemma for me, personally, and I try to recognize it when I can and give vent to my anger when it is appropriate. But beyond that, I do not always do very well with it.

QUESTION: Does life take on new meaning for you?

DR. HANLAN: I said in the article that it really didn't—I think that's what I said. My living has changed by necessity of the disease. My general or specific view of life and dying, I think, in all honesty, has not really changed very much.

QUESTION: I know what you said in the article, but I want to know the intensity of it.

DR. HANLAN: Well, I enjoy looking out that window and seeing a bare tree, and appreciating it for its own sake. A year ago, I might have thought myself nutty for contemplating a tree that much. I've had an aesthetic appreciation for nature all along, but I use that awareness now more than I had before, so that's a certain difference. I get my kicks, if you will, out of different things now, things that are within the range of possibility for me.

QUESTION: In your article, you mention, when you found out about the terminal illness, that you felt that you had cheated your children, especially your younger son. And I wonder how you feel today. And what have you done to change your relationships with your children; have you? Are there any instances that you can relate?

DR. HANLAN: I hesitate to involve my family any more than I already have in that article. Not because I think they have any big problems but because they are people in their own right. And if you want to ask them about this, fine. But I don't have a right because I am a husband and a father to publicly make use of those people. And because of some of the consequences of having that first article published, I am quite reluctant to talk about more than myself. I can spill my guts, as it were, to you about myself, but not about other people. OK? That's a cop-out, but . . .

ANSWER: That's OK; you're entitled.

DR. HANLAN: Yeah, I am.

QUESTION: Some of the experiences that you've described, I think maybe all of us have had as well, but maybe not to the same degree, the being treated as an object that you get . . . a certain hospital nonchalance about people and people's rights. Do you think there's any way that can be changed, or is this a society-wide problem or is it peculiar to hospitals or medical schools— I mean, where does it start?

DR. HANLAN: I think we have a penchant in this country, and it applies to your generation as well as to mine, for making a fad out of ideas that are not well developed or well tested. As a result of making a fad out of simple ideas, we impute a reality to our situation that then becomes self-fulfilling. For example, many people say the major problems of our society are bureaucracy and technology. And the reason for alienation among youth and among a lot of other people is that bureaucracy has become the master. Well, at one level, that's true. At another level, it's a horrible corruption of Max Weber's theory of bureaucracy, which few people know about. On the other hand, a solution some people propose is to look inside ourselves. And if we have enough self-awareness, that will solve these other problems of impersonality and being unresponsive to one another. That, I think, is, equally, a corruption of theories of Freud, and others in the sphere of economics. We have corrupted the work of Karl Marx. My point is, I think we've taken ideas and theory, corrupted them, then said this is the nature of our society and there is very little we can do about it. I don't agree with those dismal prospects. I think there is a great deal we can do, individually and collectively, to change the nature of our society. We've created that society—it didn't spring up by itself—therefore, we can change it if we want to. Specifically in the area of treating people like objects in a hospital, if we really want to, we can get people in hospitals to make sure that that simply does not happen. Or that when it happens, it is corrected. It's not that hard to get people to be humane or to stop inhumane practices. We know how to do that. Am I responding to what you asked, or not? Or am I being optimistic?

QUESTION: I'm just wondering whether it's a larger problem of how we train professionals and other people who go into helping professions in the first place, and who then have the need to help.

DR. HANLAN: I don't see our salvation, if you will, coming from the professionals. I do think there are a number of things that can be done far beyond the professionals. Again, in American society, we've made a fetish out of professionalism; particularly, the medical practitioner has more status, more rewards, more influence in this society, probably, than anywhere in the history of man. Why is that? Well, it's not just because of "those guys," it's because of us. We give them that kind of influence, and we can take that kind of influence away, I think.‡

---

‡ Editor's note: On a later occasion, Archie was asked whether he found it helpful to talk about his impending death. His answer led into this subject of professionals and training them for working with dying people:

Well, how long does one talk about dying? I have known that I am dying for two years. We all know about it all our lives. . . . Not to talk about it obviously has its problems. On the other hand, as with sex, at some point talking about it becomes utterly ridiculous. . . . A misuse of theory is the belief that talking, ventilating feelings, in itself is therapeutic. I think there is research evidence to indicate that ventilating under wrong circumstances can be quite destructive.

Beyond ventilation is required some use of psychological defenses, plus appreciation and understanding of the how and why of those defenses, and, hopefully, some psychological insight that goes beyond mere ventilation of feeling.

Of course, medical staff, skilled and unskilled, should be able to discuss dying with the patient. Yet, what is the value of my saying that? Little is to be gained by a declaration like "They must, and by God, they will!" and much destruction is risked. Sensitizing medical personnel to their own feelings about dying is important, but if that is the end of it, then all we do is reinforce the existing system through making it a bit more palatable to the health-care professional.

I think the assumed right, which is socially sanctioned, for the medical professions to unilaterally make critical decisions about patient care, and make plans for the patient, is a fundamental abuse of the philosophy of professional expertise and professional prerogative. There is, of course, a hierarchy of professional authority in medical care, with the physician at the apex of that hierarchy. There are valid reasons (such as the degree of expertise) for the physician in some situations to have a high measure of autonomy. In other situations, that kind of authority is given to the physician not only irrationally but, I think, probably illegally, in that the patient's rights are ignored. The professional is assumed a priori to know more about the patient's illness than the patient (and I don't mean to limit the critique to the physician, by any means). Therefore, there is no need to consult the patient; in fact, it is unprofessional to do so. I think we have developed a myth of professionalism in this country, particularly in the last decade or two, in which we have abandoned to the professional a variety of decision-making rights which never should have been delegated to the professional per se. Medical technology has contributed to this situation. The high degree of expertise required to be knowledgeable about the use of certain medical techniques or medical equipment broadens the gap between the professional and the patient in terms of participation of the patient in basic decisions about his life and his death.

When a patient challenges the authority of a professional, it is viewed by the professional as an affront and a personal attack because of the authority structure which defines the relationship. We have allowed this to go unchallenged for too long. A few years ago, we took our child to the hospital emergency room with an ear infection. The intern obviously did not know what he was doing, so we called a halt to the proceedings and refused to let him treat our child. We took him home. The atmosphere in that emergency room was such that we felt we had profaned the most sacred tenet in the world by saying we refused medical treatment. Apparently that was the most shocking thing that had ever occurred in that emergency room. The reaction of the nurses and doctors was that we indeed had no right to take that action. Not only that, we were made to feel that it was illegal.

How in hell did we ever allow a system to become that alienated from the needs of the people for whom it presumably exists?

And on the same occasion, he said the following:

I am sure that historically the role of the physician as soothsayer, one who controls terrible and threatening powers, not unlike the priest, has its carry-over in current practice. But obviously our society has moved far beyond witchcraft and superstition. Why do we persist, in this one area of our social institutions, to be so rooted in the Dark Ages? My own effort to answer that question suggests to me that we in the larger society are trapped in the mutually reinforcing authority system of professionals and patients,

QUESTION: How closely did you follow the stages described in Kübler-Ross? From the time you were diagnosed until now? The denial at first, and then . . . ?

DR. HANLAN: Well, one, I don't agree with the sequence of stages proposed by Kübler-Ross. Therefore, I would not apply that sequence to myself. Furthermore, she implies

---

which we are just now beginning to realize is so dysfunctional. We must begin to re-examine the entire system. In my mind, it is not simply a matter of re-educating medical personnel but a more basic action: achieving a radical redefinition of these roles. A very legalistic approach to the hospital patient's situation would, I think, have a salutary effect in the long run.

In the short run, legal action may result in some confusions and probably some retaliation against vulnerable patients, for defensiveness can lead to unintentional punishment of patients. A doctor can, for example, prescribe a test or procedure which is very painful or uncomfortable but not really needed. A nurse can ignore the call of an "offensive" patient. A physical therapist can let a patient wait an hour or two if that patient is being threatening.

My point is that the patient (particularly the terminally ill patient) is highly vulnerable in this system. Therefore, some basic reordering of the entire system is necessary. That reordering will eventually mean a major shift in the authority now carried by all members of the medical professions. I guess I agree with George Bernard Shaw as he defined professions as a "conspiracy against the laity." This was in the early part of the century. In medical care we now see the culmination of how professionalism can be abused and how professional persons can lose sight of their original goals. There is a need for physicians with considerable strength among their ranks, physicians who can delegate authority. They cannot carry the whole authority by themselves. Delegation must occur before the present terrible pressure to conform is actually broken down.

---

(From an unpublished transcription of comments made in an interview for classroom use)

that one works through the four stages and then "success-fully" arrives at a healthy, mature, desirable end of "accept-ance." Her empirical evidence for that is very, very weak, from my point of view. The reason I stress Erikson is that he does not operate from that kind of hierarchy of presumed desirable emotional states. He does not say that one ever ar-rives at a pure state of acceptance. Kübler-Ross does. That's a very old, very narrow, I think very inaccurate inter-pretation of Freudian theory, which abounds in many fields, from social work to psychiatry. I could illustrate its misuse in social work and psychology by making reference to a let-ter in a current issue of a social-work journal written. . . .*

What was overwhelming then was that they needed day care, also *special* instruction for the child, now I forget—a number of other, very realistic demands upon them—and if they would forget those problems and become "rewarding patients," who look only at their inner psyches and *accept* the child's retardation, then and only then could they get help. There are, my point is, these kinds of vicarious impli-cations in the formulation of Kübler-Ross. I don't mean to rule out or exclude completely the notion of acceptance, but in her hierarchy of stages *very* strong value judgments are imposed upon the patient. That's a long-winded answer.†

---

* Transcriber's note: End of tape inaudible. He is referring to a letter written by parents of a retarded child describing the need to "fit into" stereotyped notions of social workers and psychol-ogists in order to get aid for their child.

† Editor's note: A few months later, Archie recorded on this subject:

I would like to have Kübler Ross as a doctor in my last days or weeks. I'm sure she is a very kind and empathic per-son. I think her theories, however, are all wet. And her theory and practice have little relationship to one another. I think we have taken psychological theories and shaped them to meet our own needs. Not only Kübler-Ross but across the

QUESTION: Do you think it's possible to come to, maybe not acceptance, but a comfortable, or satisfactory to you, emotional state?

DR. HANLAN: Well, first you have to define what you think is a normal state, right? Because your question assumes that one comes to, as you say, a state that presumably, in your language or mine, is a desirable or normal state. I, for a long while, as a clinician, have not accepted *any* definition of normality. I think it is our own intention to make those of us who seem to meet the definition feel comfortable and to ward off other people who don't meet our definition. Again, the importance of Erikson's work is that you will find no use of the terms "normal" or "desirable" or "ideal" states but, rather, the view that human beings, by definition, are constantly in a state of flux. We all have our moments of irrationality, of being fearful, of freaking out if you will; we all have moments of what some would call abnormal. And we can live, I think, with very irrational fears, as many of us do. Well, I'm getting off the subject in a way, but I would strongly argue against any fixed definition of what a normal state is. I'm sure I had wider mood swings, more erratic behavior before I had terminal illness than I

---

board, we Americanize Freud and everyone else to suit ourselves. We have taken psychological theories, much as we have taken hot dogs and hamburgers, and peddled them to the masses. In the process, we have lost track of where theory is validated and where it has no validation at all. So then we say some of these theories apply . . . to death and dying simply because death and dying are becoming something to talk about in the open. And as psychobiological theories on sex were misused, we find many people unintentionally perpetuating myths about death and dying.

There's a whole new cult built on assumed knowledge about death and dying. It is the "in" thing around the country, and my concern is that the "thing" is misused in many circles simply because it is popular.

have had since that time. If you want to say I'm more normal now than I was twenty years ago, that's your privilege. I wouldn't agree. . . . The notion of normality, I think, is mixed and one that does not serve us well as human beings. Did I really answer—?

QUESTION: How do you spend your time?

DR. HANLAN: Well, I read a lot, but that's becoming more difficult. There is an article‡ coming out next week in the *Pennsylvania Gazette*, the alumni magazine, in which I say that I want to remain intellectually active as long as I can, because that's my life style, if you will. That's one of the few things I can do very actively and regularly at this point in my life. But I chose teaching as a career, and I enjoy it. And I see teaching and learning as a reciprocal kind of thing; I can't teach in any capacity unless I'm learning. It turns me on whenever I get a new idea or am stimulated by someone else. So . . . what do I do? I read, I dictate, I have classes, individual conferences with students, I rap with the students who take care of me, and I find that intellectually exciting. That's the way—

QUESTION: But is it a myth about— You often read in dramatic novels about someone who learns he has a terminal illness and suddenly they settle their business, they go to a desert island . . . and turn to doing what they've always wanted to do.

DR. HANLAN: Well, I've been doing what I've wanted to do for some while, long before I knew I had a terminal illness. I do enjoy being in the University and teaching and learning. So, there really wasn't any question about continuing what I've been doing when I found out about the disease. There are many facets of my personal life which I would like to change, but I know I can't, because I simply cannot control those factors. It wouldn't be going off to the

‡ Editor's note: "More Notes of a Dying Professor," by Archie Hanlan, *Pennsylvania Gazette* Vol. 71, No. 4 (February 1973).

Bahamas, but it might mean somehow knowing that I could pay the tuition for my children or something like that. However, those things are simply not within my ability to influence at the moment. I've learned to accept that sort of thing more than I ever thought I would. I have *never* been what you would call a patient person. I've always been impatient, wanting to do things all the time, and my illness is a harsh ruler over my impulse to try out all kinds of things, because, obviously, I'm terribly limited in what I can do. This forces me to have a kind of patience which I've never had earlier in my life. I really didn't think I could do it. But I do it pretty well.

QUESTION: Have you had to force your doctors to be honest with you? I know when I've taught medical students or worked with physicians, they pretty consistently say we don't want to tell the patient what she or he has because they're afraid they'll commit suicide or . . . this or that, and so there's the greatest reluctance to be honest.

DR. HANLAN: I have had that problem with a number of physicians. Fortunately, I do not have it with my current ones. Once, I found myself having to try to tell a doctor how he could tell another patient that he had ALS, my disease. At first, he was very shocked that I knew as much about ALS as I do. And I guess he was persuaded that if I could live with it, maybe he should reconsider telling the other patient. I frankly found it a heavy burden to try to educate him on the reasons that I thought his patient might be better off. I finally told him that the problem, from my point of view, was simply his own inability to deal with the disease and the patient who had it. I tried to say it in a way that would not be threatening or objectionable to him, because, obviously, if he were to help the other patient, I had to put it in a way he could accept. I found that *very* difficult to do. That's the last time I tried to persuade a physician on the subject.

QUESTION: Have you had any qualms about sharing your feelings so openly?

DR. HANLAN: There is a novel I'm reminded of and wanted to mention, by Dalton Trumbo, called *Johnny Got His Gun*. In that novel, the quadriplegic soldier from World War II cannot communicate at all in his hospital bed except by tapping his head. He wants the Army to put him on display, so people will see firsthand from his destroyed body the horror of war, and he thinks that his being on public display may make some people stop and think about war. Well, I don't want to be on public display. In fact, I refuse to be so. On the other hand, I share a little of Johnny's ambition in hoping that an intellectual as well as emotional discussion of my illness and my dying may make people stop and think about other ways of providing for ill people in our society. I would hope the article might have done that a little bit. If it did, then I don't mind being put on public display in that manner. I will not allow myself to be exploited, and there is the danger that I would make a kind of profession of dying, and I think that could become quite offensive too. I have to have something more of value for you and for myself beyond the mere fact that I know I have an incurable disease.

QUESTION: Did you find in hospitals that the actual quality of physical care varied in any way for the unrewarding patient?

DR. HANLAN: Unrewarding patients, I think very often quite unintentionally, get punished. I remember an elderly woman sent to a lab when I was there. She was in a wheelchair and quite confused and possibly senile. When they took her out of the wheelchair for the exam, they found a bedpan glued to her buttocks. It obviously had been there for a day or more. The neglect which that represents must reflect her being seen as an unrewarding patient. I could cite other, gorier examples, but I won't.

MRS. TAYLOR: There was a study done on nurses and their response to the call buttons of patients who are dying and to the call buttons of other patients. They found that it took almost twice as long for the nurses to answer the call buttons of the dying patients. And I'm sure, when the nurses were confronted with it, it was very much a subconscious or unconscious thing: they had to finish this chart, or they had to pour this medication, and they would get to it. But in reality, it took them twice as long.

DR. HANLAN: I talked with a patient some while ago who has a terminal disease and was in the hospital—she may be dead by now. One of the things she said is, "Nobody holds my hand." Which is quite a story in itself. What I think she was saying is that she knew she was an unrewarding patient but that someone should hold her hand anyway.

MRS. TAYLOR: One of the things I think also at work is that we tend to be such a task-oriented society, and medical people so often define their tasks by what can I do, what injection can I give, what medication can I give, what physical thing can I do—without any comprehension that a great deal can be done in the holding of hands or just being present.

[Pause]

DR. HANLAN: OK. Was I really so scary?

[Laughter.]

COMMENT: I'm impressed, from the last time I was here to this time, with how much more at ease you seem to be. I see a real change in your spirit and much more ease with what's happening to you.

DR. HANLAN: Maybe a greater acceptance.

[Laughter.]

COMMENT: No matter how defined.

DR. HANLAN: Your point is probably terribly accurate, because I went through a real personal crisis a week or so after you last saw me, one that had probably been building but which I was not aware of when I saw you. (And that bears on one of my general points: that none of us, at any one point in time, have everything figured out or have all the answers for our own lives. We constantly rework them. And life is a series of crises and conflicts to be dealt with and lived with and lived through. I'm only saying what I've had to learn or relearn myself in recent months.)

DR. SCHMITT: Having heard you lecture three times, I'd say I've had an impact that says simply: if Archie can do it, I can do it; so that, it's been of tremendous therapeutic value to me to have sat here with you on three occasions; you've shared so freely with us that . . . it's really given me a kind of courage and I say, "Well, that's not the worst thing there is. Why this terrible fear of dying in America?" One way of abating this fear is just daring to stick close to somebody, and witnessing your daring to share yourself with people. I think there's help in all of these aspects.

DR. HANLAN: And, in that sense, you and the rest of the group have helped me, too. . . . I really look forward to each of these meetings. It's the high point of the semester for *me*.

Well, how about that?

MRS. TAYLOR: One of the things you said last time that I found tremendously meaningful was that you're terminally ill but that you don't want to be called a dying patient, because you're very much about the business of living.

DR. HANLAN: Right.

I guess the moral of this story is that I got more help in one session with a psychotherapist in November, more help than I thought I got. I knew I was helped at the time, but I didn't think it would show. I would strongly encourage any or all of you not to fear getting professional help. And if you don't like the person who is helping you, don't stay with him. Get someone else. I have found it beneficial, but I'm also highly selective in deciding who I think can really help me.

[Pause]

DR. SCHMITT: Is that a closure that's felt in the room? I think maybe we should terminate, and thanks a lot, Archie. From here on in, for the rest of the course, the students will always come back to Archie and quote. . . . You will be very much a live part of our course on dying; that's the impact you have made in this course.

ARCHIE J. HANLAN, D.S.W.

# A Life Line of Students

The smell of newly finished cement, sawdust, and sweaty bodies commingled in a crowded elevator of "Highrise South." The university "Superblocks" were being occupied for the first time, and students and their parents were arriving from all over the East Coast. The people in the elevator were a microcosm of the University. Above the hum of the ascending elevator, I could clearly hear the voice of a doting mother reassuring herself to her son that they had brought everything he would need for his apartment. His silent and harassed-looking father was quite identifiable by his sullen glances at the boy's mother. William Smith III, as I will call him, was the epitome of what the Ivy League freshman must have looked like even a hundred years ago. He was dressed in a blazer, tie, and well-pressed slacks, and groomed in a manner that spelled eighteen long years of parental effort. The mother's conversation told us that they had just arrived after a weary journey from upstate New York.

They got off the elevator with me at the nineteenth floor. I am sure that scene was duplicated hundreds of times that day by other freshmen and their parents. The reason, however, that this all remains vivid in my memory lies in what I saw on the following day: As I was waiting for the elevator to take me downstairs, a sloppy and unclean-looking youth ambled alongside me to await the elevator. He greeted me in an open and casual manner. His hair was disheveled. He wore Indian beads around his bare chest and an Indian headband. His frayed shorts exposed hairy legs and clumsy bare feet. The shock came on gradually, as I realized this was my shattered illusion of the Ivy League young man whose parents had left him here the day before. I found myself mentally reciting all of the stereotypes about irresponsible and juvenile college students personified in this young man's appearance. I had no notion that two years thence my life would literally depend upon similar Penn students.

That is the story I want to tell you. By the fall of 1972, my terminal illness had progressed to the point where it was necessary that someone be with me all of the time. I was able to teach full time but was restricted to a wheelchair, with my arms rapidly becoming paralyzed. My wife and I decided to try to hire students at Penn to help me during the day.

Three students stayed with me Monday through Friday from eight to five o'clock for the entire fall semester. At that time, I was going to the University about two days a week and having one seminar held in my home off campus.

I will use pseudonyms for the students and intentionally give some misleading information about them. First, Larry is a nineteen-year-old pre-med student. He grew up in an affluent Philadelphia suburb. His conservative Jewish parents were in the process of a divorce when I first met Larry.

Second, Ann is a twenty-five-year-old graduate student in the humanities. During several years abroad with the Peace Corps, she began to question her midwestern Catholic upbringing, but she remains committed to a highly rigorous set of ethics and values.

Third, Ronald is a twenty-one-year-old senior in business administration. He views himself as coming straight out of a Philip Roth novel about a middle-class Jewish family from New York.

If you were to see any one of these students, your attention might be drawn to them because of their non-conformist dress and appearance. You might be startled as I was when I saw the young man in the high-rise dormitory. Larry, Ann, and Ronald might provoke in you some of the negative, stereotyped notions about irresponsible college students. What I hope to be able to do here is to help you look beyond their superficial appearance, and see the unique human beings beneath that surface.

I do not believe I have ever seen Ann in a dress. Her usual costume was a nondescript shirt and jeans. She saw makeup as part of a false value system. The only adornment to her face was a pair of large, wire-rimmed glasses. Ann's physical appearance hardly suggested a graduate scholar; she is one of the very brightest students I have known.

Larry looks like a figure out of a Picasso painting with his long curly hair, curly beard, and beat-up clothing. As with the other students, Larry's appearance reveals very little about his social status and background. I doubt that many of you could envision Larry assuming responsibility for your medical care. If you came to this conclusion, however, you would have done yourself a grave injustice.

Of the three students, Ronald's appearance is by far the most dramatic. He has long, flowing, blond hair, which in itself evokes a wide range of reactions. I was able to see these reactions firsthand when Ronald would push me in my wheelchair around the campus. I doubt that many people noticed that Ronald actually was a rather conservative dresser, wearing very neat shirts and slacks. His bare feet undid any impression of conventionality. My guess is that many of you would think of Ronald as bringing down the Establishment, although, from experience with him, I am persuaded that he is much more likely to become a successful and socially responsible entrepreneur.

My wife and I had long interviews with each student before we made a joint decision. We rarely disagreed. Many who applied were much too frightened and uncomfortable about my disability and illness. Their efforts to cover up their discomfort were obvious to both of us. Larry seemed to go to the opposite extreme. He appeared to be brash and quite unaffected. Obviously, a great deal of this was bravado. I remember his saying that he could make fantastic sandwiches. If he could, he never demonstrated that ability to me. However, Larry had other talents.

One of the things Larry could do very well was to feed me, much as an infant is fed, without needing to joke or deprecate himself or me in the process. He could take me to the bathroom without embarrassment. The only thing in the daily routine which really seemed to bother him was brushing my hair. All he said about it was that he never had brushed another man's hair before. An ordinary day with me has many frustrations and some occasional fear that I might fall or otherwise hurt myself. Larry's whimsical sense poked fun at some of these situations without making either of us the butt of his humor.

Larry was trying to get straight A's to ensure his admittance to a medical school. This meant that he frequently studied until 3:00 or 4:00 A.M. He would show up at my house at eight o'clock, still in a fog. He was very careful and thorough in helping me get ready for my class, and he stayed with me in the classroom. He sat next to me in front of the class. One day, after I had been lecturing for about fifteen minutes, I turned to look at Larry, and he was not there. I looked around the room and finally saw him sprawled out on the floor sound asleep. I later learned that his exhaustion was not solely from studying. He was keeping a mistress and that accounted for at least some of his weariness.

Larry would probably be disappointed at my reference to his "keeping a mistress," because that phrase represents the language and values of my generation and not of his. The almost universal characteristic of young people I have met at Penn is their painfully honest and open relationships with one another. Sexual liaisons and love affairs are not subject to ridicule or to any implication of the old double standard. In any event, Larry made no secret of living with his girl friend, and he took his responsibility for the relationship very seriously. I can think of many marriages in my generation which are much more superficial and much less humane.

The preceding narrative was begun two months ago. It has been interrupted a number of times because of the progression of my illness. Most of my speech is now unintelligible, and even the effort to speak exhausts me. It is evident that I cannot finish the article. I am tempted to try to say all the things that I would like to say in one brief summary. I recognize, of course, that this is impossible.

I had intended to develop the interaction between me and these students as illustrations of the interdependent and reciprocal nature of human intercourse. I would not have portrayed the students as paragons of virtue, but I would have indicated that their search for identity and meaning on their own terms and without false idols is an effort we should all recognize and respect. The refusal to accept traditional values and ethics simply because they are propounded by organized religion or by our dominant social and political institutions places a burden on these young people to establish firmly for themselves precisely what their own values are or should be. As one student plaintively asked me, "Then, what are the important values, and where do they come from?" Such values are obviously not to be found in current national political leadership. Some of that leadership has openly advocated distrust and hostility toward the very young people who are trying to articulate basic human values to be acted on in all areas of our lives.

I am not suggesting that these young people have found the answers. Indeed, I could give you examples of how confused and inconsistent they are at times. But they have served me extraordinarily well and have helped make my last year of academic life stimulating and rewarding.

In February 1973, Archie and Mary were invited to present material at Grand Rounds, Presbyterian Hospital, Philadelphia. Exhausted from the last seminar on death and dying, he found he could not manage it. Mary appeared alone and addressed the group, from both her point of view and his, on problems that they had encountered with his medical care.

That spring, he conducted only one class, the doctoral seminar begun in the fall. He continued individual conferences with students, but he no longer went to the campus.

When the *Delaware Medical Journal* requested an article, he prepared the following paper, reprinted with permission of its publishers. Archie was pleased with the opportunity to address a group of physicians. The article was published after his death, in February of 1974. *Philadelphia Medicine* reprinted it the following June.

He recorded this article very much as if the audience were actually present. It is with this "conversation," so to speak, that we conclude the book.

M.N.

ARCHIE J. HANLAN, D.S.W.

# A Patient's View of
# Amyotrophic Lateral Sclerosis

For the last two years, since I have known that I have the incurable disease of ALS, I have lectured and written about my experience as a dying patient (*Pennsylvania Gazette*, March 1972, February 1973). As the disease has progressed, I have become concerned with more than simply telling an emotional story, and I have become acutely aware of the need for a rational and critical evaluation of medical care in general and of the plight of the dying patient in particular. I hope that this paper, intended for a medical audience, will be read and considered not as a personal attack but, rather, as an effort to articulate a perspective that is necessarily quite different from that of the physician.

What I think I know that few of you know is what it is really like to be a dying patient in the network of our medical system. I am not questioning or judging the medical knowledge and skill of the physician; yet, I have had to learn the hard way that some physicians are not well informed about ALS. Let me give you an example of how it

NOTE: The author wants to acknowledge the help of his wife and Donald Berman in preparing this manuscript and of Drs. Gertrude and Reuben Copperman for their support and suggestions.

took me several months to discover that one of my previous doctors was not able to give me accurate information regarding one aspect of the disease.

Early in my illness, I would fall down frequently. One evening, I fell flat on my back in my bedroom. My wife was unable to move me and we were both very frightened for several hours. At precisely the same time, I became impotent for the first time in my life. I went to a physician to try to clarify if my sudden impotence was disease-related or partly psychological. When I described my problem to the physician, he was obviously startled by my frank discussion of the problem and finally stammered out that he had never been asked that kind of question before. I do not expect doctors to be free of sexual inhibition, but I do expect them to know relevant physiological information on sexual functioning. It was not until some time later, when sexual functioning had returned spontaneously, that I learned that this physician had been misinformed on the subject.

The same doctor described above asked for my advice in telling another patient about her diagnosis of ALS. The doctor at first found it very hard to believe that I knew my diagnosis and prognosis, refusing to respond to my efforts to engage him in a discussion of the disease. When he realized that my understanding of the disease was fairly accurate, he then haltingly told me about his woman patient. I tried to find out from him how much the patient did know. He was obviously unclear about what he had told the patient during the past several months. I commented that surely she must have put some of the information together for herself. He agreed, but argued that few people could tolerate the full knowledge about such a disease, with the implication that I was a rather strange and inexplicable exception to the rule. I then suggested that sometimes the difficulty in facing the disease lies as much or more with the doctor as with the patient. I had gone too far with this man and that ended his discussion of the subject. I have not tried since then to persuade physicians about discussing diagnoses and terminal illness.

I make a critical distinction between the expertise of the physician and the administrative exercise of that expertise in our health-care system. Thus, I present the view of a patient who feels trapped in a system by well-intentioned medical personnel, and where there is not any simple blame that can be assigned to any one group. Our movies and television notwithstanding, there are really not good guys and bad guys, but, rather, there are organizational and social structures that envelop all of us regardless of our intentions. It is in these areas that I think that I can attempt some analysis that may have some benefit beyond the limited scope of any one doctor or patient.

One of the most important structural features of medical care in our society is that of the bureaucratic and hierarchical ordering of authority within and among professions and between professionals and patients. The problem is by no means limited to medicine, since it is a common complaint about all areas of our society. A Harvard professor of government, Hoffman, has analyzed our malaise as a growing crisis of the legitimacy of all our social institutions. But, again, our concern here is how these larger social events penetrate the quality and quantity of life for the patient.

An example of an unintended trauma related to bureaucratic medical authority comes from my own experience: The morning after I was informed of my diagnosis of ALS, I was asked to appear before a large class of medical students. I was aware that I could refuse, but at the same time I felt I might make a small contribution in medical education. I have often been on the other side of the fence—that is, observing medical and psychiatric patients for teaching and research purposes. At any rate, I agreed to be on display for the benefit of the medical students.

Already in a state of near exhaustion, as described in

the *Gazette* article, I was ordered to go to the classroom in a wheelchair. When I protested that I could walk perfectly well, I was given some no-nonsense reply leaving me no other choice. The class was conducted by my physician, a professor of medicine to whom great deference was shown by the promptness and efficiency with which I was delivered to the classroom. It was a strange experience to be in front of the classroom not as the professor but as a patient stared upon by a mass of immobile faces. Profaning the role expected of me, I made some occasional bantering comments. The doctor's austere ignoring of my comments at least told the students what he thought was the proper behavior there. He frequently referred to me in the third person. Because of the rare nature of my disease and the fact that I was in a very early stage, the whole event took on an atmosphere of one-upmanship regarding the diagnosis. At least while I was present, none of the students seemed to come close to the diagnosis, and this pleased the professor. As the question-and-answer period came close to the overt discussion of my illness, the professor promptly thanked me and had me removed from the room. On reflection, it seems about as juvenile as allowing a child to remain in an adult conversation about sex, only to be removed when the language is made explicit. The child, and the patient, have long since figured out what is being talked about, but now the subject is made taboo, forbidden, and often terrifying.

The guessing game about my illness made me wonder at times what in the hell I was doing there. It was as though the disease entity itself were much more important than me, the patient. I found myself remembering that I had just been told that my world was coming to an end, so why was I allowing myself to take part in this fantasy? At that point, I could not withdraw from the classroom, and the anger I felt about the incident remained smoldering within me for a long while after. One day, the world was my oyster. The next day, it all came crashing down. And I felt like an inanimate specimen prepared on a slide for viewing by unknown doctors.

To me, this illustrates the complex problem of making changes in medical education. These medical students and I were forced into traditional role models. For example, the professor who had me before his class was non-verbally teaching his students how to behave in an objective and impersonal manner with a patient with a catastrophic illness. If those students were at all representative, they reflected back very well their objectivity and distance from the patient. We often underestimate the amount of imitation and socialization that occur in our educational system. The student's rebellion and criticism of this learning process is often more ephemeral than the behavior taught by the instructor himself. In my case, a great deal was taught the students about the proper roles of doctor and patient.

Let me give another personal example of the system of health care's assuming a life of its own quite apart from the need of the patient and the doctor. I was hospitalized in a special medical evaluation unit for an assessment of my disease and for occupational-therapy devices. This unit was uniquely designed to focus twenty-four-hour care on the individual needs of each patient. The staff and facilities were exceptional. I specify all of this because it dramatizes some incredible events that occurred in spite of all the best intentions. I shared a room with an elderly retired man who was recovering from a stroke. It took me three days to realize that he and I were being subjected to a peculiar form of discrimination in the unit. Of a total of about twenty patients, he and I were the first to be awakened every morning and the last to be served breakfast. We were the most disabled patients on the ward and that might have provided some rationale for taking more time with us in the morning. It did not justify, however, getting us up at six o'clock, putting us in wheelchairs by ourselves, and then not serving us breakfast until nine o'clock. Most other patients were not awakened before seven o'clock and they were served breakfast by eight o'clock. I really couldn't believe that this was happening to us, but I finally reported it directly to the medical director of the unit.

The next day, my roommate and I were not awakened until seven o'clock. The nurse in charge of that shift acidly commented to me that I must enjoy the extra hour of sleep in the morning. Her comment indicated very clearly to me that although my complaint had been remedied, the reason for the complaint obviously was not dealt with. I did not want an extra hour's sleep. I did want to be treated like a human being and not unnecessarily differentiated from the other patients. This point seemed to have completely escaped the nurse.

On the third day, my personal physician came to visit me at the hospital. I was feeling the full rage of the discriminating treatment by this time. A student nurse had been assigned to me for the entire day as part of her learning. She was with me when my doctor arrived. I exclaimed, "Reuben, this place is a monstrosity"; I could almost feel the student nurse shudder. She moved behind me, out of my vision. Within a minute or two, she disappeared and I never saw her again. Obviously, that student had not been told that patients sometimes get angry and may express that anger in harmless verbal statements. Whatever the reasons for her reactions, at that point in time they only reinforced my feeling of being trapped by a monolithic system over which I could exercise very little influence. And this feeling of being manipulated by the system was not lessened, even though I had direct access to the medical director.

Let me try to use another physician to illustrate what I mean by both doctor and patient being trapped in the network of our medical system. Another medical friend told me of the importance of getting regular physical therapy as soon as possible. My physician at this time practiced in a large hospital that had outstanding physical- and occupational-therapy facilities. A month went by after my request for a referral to the Physical Therapy Department, and I finally contacted someone in that department directly. I was told that they received no referral from my doctor. Going back to him, he said a referral had been made but apparently it had been lost along the way. Another month went by, and my disease progressed. This time, I obtained information that required that I circumvent the medical authority of my doctor in that hospital. What I then learned was that my doctor made the referral to another doctor who did not think that there was any point in someone with my condition receiving physical therapy. The view was that what good would it do anyway, since the disease was advancing rapidly? There then followed a ridiculous procedure of intrigue and behind-the-scene effort to get physical therapy for me at my own home. I still cannot believe that my doctor really intended to prevent me from getting the physical therapy, but he and I became locked into a network of relationships that made our working together impossible. Fortunately, I had other medical alternatives, which few patients have.

Let me give a more positive illustration of a physician who responded to me in a very different way. Sometime after the initial diagnosis, I sought a confirming evaluation by another specialist. He confirmed the diagnosis of ALS. In telling me this, he told me with great feeling that he wondered at times why he ever went into this specialty. Tears came to his eyes. What he was conveying to me was his frustration at the limits of his medical knowledge and skill, baring his own sense of inadequacy and impotence in the face of this disease. Even more important, he was conveying to me my importance as a human being. As maudlin or simplistic as this may seem, the value of this rare kind of honesty cannot be overestimated when one has encountered too many other physicians who can only handle their own feelings by withdrawal, denial, and making the patient feel that his own self-worth has somehow become suddenly and permanently discredited.

Fortunately, there are a number of doctors that I can cite from my own personal experience who have gone far beyond the most demanding interpretation of the Hippocratic oath. For example, my personal physician has made endless home calls, thoroughly reviewed all published research on the disease, and somehow has managed to meet my medical needs as the total devastation of the disease runs its course. I could give many other examples of how some members of the medical profession, in the face of an inability to extend the quantity of my life, have contributed to the more important aspects of improving the quality of my life.

My motivation for addressing myself to you, however, is not to indulge in a superficial extolling of the virtues of your profession. Rather, I am driven by a great need to somehow communicate a different way of looking at your practice of medicine, which may aid your perceiving other patients in a different light. Your profession alone cannot change the nature of our medical-care system. The best I can hope is that some insight derived from my own experience may heighten the awareness of some others.

The course of my disease has made it necessary for me to have twenty-four-hour surveillance and care. I am still living at home, when most patients at this point are institutionalized. Other ALS patients have written to me describing their experience with starvation and malnutrition, with unnecessary atrophy of muscles for lack of help in obtaining any exercise, and for the incredible exhaustion that the disease places on family members. It also has to be noted that some physicians simply abandon the patient and the family as the disease reaches total disability.

While the nature of the disease demands constant adjustment by the patient to his deteriorating physical condition, there are reactions I have had in the most recent stages that I did not anticipate. I did expect the increasing disability to sharpen my conflicts about being psychologically and physically dependent. I did not foresee, however, the extent to which I would feel a kind of emotional regression forced upon me, a kind of infantilizing of all aspects of my life. For example, because of my increased speech defect I am sometimes talked to or about in the third person. As a result, I have no doubt that my frustration level is markedly reduced and that my intolerance for ambiguity is painfully apparent.

My contact with the outside world is always mediated by someone else now. Again, the major burden falls on my family, especially on my wife. My own involvement in all of the small and large decisions that have to be made about me becomes necessarily constricted. I already know too well, from my earlier hospitalizations, that my own participation in decision-making requires my constant vigilance and initiative. It seems inevitable that others in the medical system will move toward encapsulating me from an active role in the critical decisions that remain to be made.

I recognize that any redistribution of medical authority is a very complex matter, and I am concerned that the efforts of well-intentioned reformers can often backfire, with unintended consequences for the patient. Therefore, I am hesitant to suggest the implementation of either an aggressive legal enforcement of patients' rights or of a radical and sudden delegation of authority to paraprofessionals. I find this personally to be something of a dilemma. It seems necessary to me that patients will have to continue for a long while to rely on the humane and judicious use of discretion which is in the hands of the physician.

Having arrived at the above analysis and conclusions, it has been apparent to me that if my own experience with an incurable disease is to have any significance at all, it would be the effort to somehow communicate aspects of our medical system in which we all become mutually dependent. My criticism is not of the medical profession or of doctors per se.

Yet, you are in a unique position to exert some influence on that system in behalf of the patient. As difficult as my situation is, I really do not envy the position in which your practice often puts you. The most that I can ask of you is that you listen and weigh what I and other patients have to say. That in itself is more helpful than you may imagine.